The poems of
Valentin Iremonger

The poems of
Valentin Iremonger

Edited by Seán Haldane

RÚN POCKET POEMS

Published in 2014 by Rún Press Limited, Cork, Ireland.

www.runepress.ie

Printed and bound in Great Britain by
TJ International Ltd., Padstow, Cornwall.

Book design by Bite Design, Cork

ISBN: 978-0-9574669-4-4

All in the end
for Sheila naturally

Iremonger's dedication to his wife Sheila Manning, in Horan's Field

Contents

Horan's Field and Other Reservations

Uncollected poems

Versions and translations

Poems in Irish

Wrap Up My Green Jacket

Introduction

Valentin Iremonger (1918 – 1991) is the quiet man of 20th century Irish poetry in English. He is mentioned occasionally in political biographies (e.g. Conor Cruise O'Brien's *Memoir: My Life and Themes*) as a civil servant and diplomat. In literary history he is on the margins: his help with Old Irish tree lore was acknowledged by Robert Graves in the Foreword to *The White Goddess*; he had a notorious row with P J Kavanagh who accused him of being the author of an article in a newspaper against which Kavanagh took out and failed in a libel action; he made Brendan Behan famous through his recommendation of *Borstal Boy* to a London publisher; and he wrote critical essays for Seán Ó Faoláin at *The Bell*, where a verse play on Robert Emmet was published, subsequently finding its way to a BBC radio performance.

Although Iremonger wrote his name as Valentin, he had been baptised Valentine and pronounced it that way. He was known to family and friends as Val.

As a diplomat living with his family abroad (First Secretary in Britain, Ambassador in Sweden, India, and Luxembourg), Iremonger was in no position to promote his poems, but nor was it his temperament to do so. In 1979 he had a fall which caused a traumatic brain injury. This necessitated surgery to the front of his skull, and he suffered typical symptoms of 'frontal' injury, including loss of initiative and social withdrawal. These symptoms have been wrongly attributed to alcohol misuse – not uncommon in embassies with lavish drink budgets, and it was probably not wise to go drinking with Brendan Behan – but until the injury he had

sustained a busy life as diplomat, family man, and poet. In 1980
he had to retire from Foreign Affairs. His life as a writer had also
stopped, although he continued to read.

I came across his work in 1962 in an Oxford bookshop. The book
was *The Dolmen*, a 'miscellany of Irish writing', which contained
three of his poems, including 'Invocation' with its theme of waiting
for inspiration, which was the subject of Robert Graves's lectures
at the time, and translations of two poems by an unknown Breton
French poet, René Guy Cadou. (Here one remarkable but not
well known poet had discovered another: only recently, long after
his death, has Cadou come into his own in the canon of French
poetry). Iremonger, who was Irish attaché in London, attended a
lecture given by Graves that year. What remains of one side of their
earlier correspondence from 1943 to 1948, only a few letters from
Iremonger, is now among the Graves papers at St John's College,
Oxford. Iremonger had started by sending Graves some of his
poems, and then wrote: 'You were generous, you know: I suppose
I did know all about them, as you say, before I sent them – but it
is very helpful to have another's opinion.' This opinion apparently
included pointing out some 'rhetoric', but if Graves liked a person's
poems, he opened up on other things. Iremonger continued: 'If,
as you say, poetry is a sharing of secrets, today these secrets are
proscribed and it is not by shouting and tearing one's hair or by
roaring through a microphone they will be shared.' And 'We have
lost the capacity to "see real miracles" as Laura Riding [Graves's
former companion and Muse] says. One of war's results seems to
be that poets make a frontal assault on Truth and attempt to state,
beyond yea or nay, general definitions and moral judgements. To me
this doesn't seem to be the poet's job.'

Iremonger's own poems show the attachment to what Blake
called 'the minute particular' which defines poetry also for
Graves. And in keeping with the urgency of Ó Faoláin and other

contributors to *The Bell* about Irish literature having to be realistic and to turn its back on the Celtic Twilight created by such as Yeats and AE, Iremonger wrote to Graves (who loathed Yeats) that 'the huge Celtic fabric built up by Yeats and his disciples was fake. It couldn't stand up to an economic depression, much less armour-piercing bombs.' But later in 1944 he wrote to Graves about 'what you indicate is our only salvation – the elements of myth: the gods and goddesses, the ghouls and ghosts, beast, bird, fish, roots.' He also referred to the Welsh poet Alun Lewis whose poems, after his death, had been edited by Graves: 'Lewis, honouring the sacrificial rites of his country.… Here in Ireland we cannot so readily accept the mythology… The currency of our sagas has been debased by Yeats, AE, and the remainder of that and the succeeding generations who followed their lead. For my own part I feel that I must fight it and conquer it first.'

This was a fairly subtle position: Iremonger at the age of 26 rejected the fakery of the Celtic Twilight in favour of realism, yet still looked for something in mythology. It must also be remembered that his Irish was already good from school and university in Dublin, and it would become excellent as he learned more from his wife Sheila Manning's family in the Kerry Gaeltacht and began to write in Munster Irish. (Yeats knew very little Irish.) Iremonger and his wife also participated in modernistic theatre productions, both in Dublin and in the often experimental Lyric Theatre in Belfast. And all in all, Iremonger's position in his essays for *The Bell,* taking off from his correspondence with Graves, was not likely to make him popular:

> Mules have nothing on poets when it comes to stubbornness; and the efforts of others to direct the writings of poets have always met with the equivalent of the Dubliner's exasperated "Who d'ya think you're shoving?" So that if my work has

tended (as a friend said) to become less concerned with
general definitions and moral judgments and more concerned
with the apparently trivial and insignificant (a girl on a
bed noticing Spring, a childhood memory, a chance phrase
thrown against my ears in the street, a walk up the garden, a
girl on a mountain tying her scarf, saying, "I'm going down")
all I will say is, with Dedalus, 'Signatures of all things I am
here to read.'

Later in the same passage, Iremonger refers, as in his letter to
Graves, to poetry as an 'encirclement movement' and concludes that
'It is doubtful if the classical acceptance of what we call "evil" is ever
possible again, yet without this acceptance we cannot even begin to
see life in the round.' And again, 'Poetry is the sharing of secrets, of
secrets that today are proscribed. This proscription makes it more
difficult now than at any previous time to write freely, and it is the
sense of oppression, of impending disaster, that accounts for the
rhetoric that fogs so much contemporary verse.'

This is not the tone of a future diplomat! His poems, too,
although often quietly spoken, show a disturbing realism and detail –
and, yes, a sense of evil, with no consoling fakery.

This introduction will not examine Iremonger's poems or the few
critical comments that exist about them. The poems, to use a phrase
Iremonger applied in a review, are from 'the only place where poetry
can be found – in the everyday life of the people around [the poet]'.
And they speak for themselves, in a particular voice. Ó Faoláin said
of Irish poetry of his time that 'one rarely hears a modern idiom, a
modern speech. (I find it in the tense poetry of W R Rodgers and in
the hesitating rhythm of Valentin Iremonger).' For myself, I am most
impressed by how long Iremonger's sentences are: his poems are the
epitome of 'feeling thought'.

As for the critical comments, they fall short of being genuine criticism, as when Dennis O'Driscoll, who concludes that Iremonger deserves 'a modest space on the bookshelf', is bothered by 'a sombre recess of the psyche', by 'fearful rather than cheerful anticipation', and by 'youthful despondencies': in other words, by an absence of the rhetorical fog of optimism. It seems that the secrets are still proscribed if they entail facing a reality that may be gloomy. And 'the rest of his meagre output consisted mainly of wilful efforts to revive his old afflatus.' Which is precisely what Iremonger never gave into: when his inspiration stopped, he stopped. If he had only so many poems in him, well then, that was what he had. But even his manuscript poem, 'By the Waters of Yamuna', although gloomy – it's about death, after all – asserts something about life:

> …their eyes filled
> Not with despair – like hope here irrelevant –
> But a dubious trust, each day renewed,
> In simple survival….

Every age has its flash poets. And every age has its quiet poets who win through in the long run. (Think of Clare as distinct from Shelley, Hardy as distinct from Tennyson.) As the poet (in Irish) Máire Mhac an tSaoi put it after his death, 'Valentin Iremonger, both as a poet and as a human being, radiated integrity.' Iremonger, not only as an Irish poet in English but as an English poet in the older linguistic sense, and briefly as an Irish poet in Irish, takes his place in a few dozen remarkable poems. And the less remarkable poems still have something to say. Valentin Iremonger is a real poet for real times – or if the times are not real, for real readers.

Seán Haldane

A note on the text

This aims to be a complete collection of Iremonger's poems, published and unpublished, although it is possible (and to be hoped) that further unpublished poems may one day appear from lost letters or manuscripts.

Most of these poems were published in:
> On The Barricades (with Robert Greacen and
> Bruce Williamson), Dublin, 1944
> Reservations, London, 1950
> Horan's Field and Other Reservations, Dublin, 1972
> Sandymount, Dublin, 1988.

His early poems had appeared in *The Bell* and *Envoy* (which he briefly edited). Some poems were published in all four volumes above. In this collection, they are in chronological order insofar as this can be established from these volumes. If a poem that appears in an early volume appears in revised form in a later volume, then it will appear under that volume. But almost all poems contain no revisions after their first publication.

There is no section for *Sandymount* since it is a selection of 40 poems already published in the previous three volumes (which contain 68 poems in all, excluding translations).

The procedure has been followed of titling sections according to the book in which the poem first appeared, with separate sections for 'Uncollected Poems' (poems from manuscript or published in periodicals but not in books), and for the verse play *Wrap up my Green Jacket*.

Some of the play *Wrap up my Green Jacket* is in prose, but it contains passages of poetry that could stand on their own as poems but which are best understood in their original context.

Wrap up my Green Jacket was broadcast twice by the BBC in 1947, produced by Louis MacNeice, with a cast including Cyril Cusack and Betty Chancellor, and with ballads arranged by Iremonger's wife Sheila Manning.

The poem 'This ivory-handled knife', and the two translations from René Guy Cadou, appeared in *The Dolmen, miscellany of Irish writing*, Dublin and London, 1962.

It can be noted that Iremonger's verse translation of Rilke's *Das Marienleben* into Irish verse, *Beatha Mhuire* (1955) is not included in this collection.

The text of the two Poems in Irish is as given in *Sandymount*. *In Memoriam* is translated by Seán Haldane, *Dán* by Torlach Mac Con Midhe.

Acknowledgments

This book could not have happened without the emotional commitment of its copyright holders, Valentin Iremonger's three daughters, Avril Iremonger, Catherine Webb, and Susan Iremonger, and his daughter-in-law, Vitsomeno Iremonger.

We are also grateful for help to Mark and Cian Iremonger, Barry Iremonger, Bridget Hourican, and three librarians: Stewart Tiley, St John's College, Oxford; Crónán Ó Doibhlin, University College, Cork; and especially Gearóid Ó Luing, National Library of Ireland. Thanks also to Poetry Ireland Review for access to rare issues.

Thanks to David Cameron and Torlach Mac Con Midhe for advice on English and Irish texts. And thanks to Aron Lawton-Wright for help with photographs.

On The
Barricades
1944

WELL, I DECLARE

So many of them, in their impressive attitudes,
Standing under the architraves of the day and the night,
Have spoken pointedly to us and with concern,

Splitting the hairs of logic, that all turned sour
On the tongues of our minds and our eyes wandered
Like schoolchildren's under the earnest teacher,

And it appears now to us that there is no justification
Either for optimism or pessimism as they discuss

The metaphysical necessity for the historical approach,

Who have cheated us for our houses and the broad acres
Our fathers designed for us, leaving us only
The leaking barns and doss-houses of our future.

Let us resolve, then, each, not to be put upon,
To have no truck with anger or apathy, to accept
No man's word for anything: not even for God:
Not even our own.

BACKWARD LOOK

Looking at stones and airguns I recall my childhood
Spent among tin-cans, gravel-heaps and dead walls,
And the strand at Sandymount, where the tide reminded
Me of the outside newspaper world.

But my world was private and immense enough then:
Its statesmen had torn jerseys and great vocabularies,
Though the words that hurtled from their mouths were the parents'
    fears

Pathologically transmitted to their sons
Who herded together in armies and elected leaders
And were instinctively kind in their frequent wars:
Being anxious about the wounded, abandoning hostilities
When pellets or stones or sods of grass drew tears.

The depredation of orchards was the intuitive beginning
Of the later scramble for food; though the well-earned fruits were
    communal:
Sharing of profits being the natural order of things
In that world where our hopes were neighbours and friendly.

These now are gibbering days. My head is in iron.
I walk around in a rank and dare not break it.
My minutes move on to a fate they cannot retard.
I look at the gun they have given me and am sad.

THE TOY HORSE

Somebody, when I was young, stole my toy horse,
The charm of my morning romps, my man's delight.
For two days I grieved, holding my sorrow like flowers
Between the bars of my sullen angry mind.

Next day I went out with evil in my heart,
Evil between my eyes and at the tips of my hands,
Looking for my enemy at the armed stations,
Until I found him, playing in his garden

With my toy horse, urgent in the battle
Against the enemies of his Unreason's land:
He was so happy, I gave him also
My vivid coloured crayons and my big, glass marble.

ALONE BY NIGHT

In the room, between the lamplight and the door's shadow,
My fear stands monstrous as a naked man,
Clutching the night of the air like a brief cudgel
Over the turmoil of my bleeding past.

I have forgotten how the bright girls danced
Here with a rustle of skirts and a soft laugh.
It is so long since they left this castle,
Not liking the dross and the dirt of its unswept halls.

My eyes follow only the lurching movements
Of this ill-shaped fury, this mountainous bawd,
Who has jumped the claim of my joy and laughter
And frightened away the happy girls.

Between the two eyes I shot him several times
And went back to my books and picked up my pen.
But before nightfall he was capering before me,
More insistent and ugly with the angry wounds.

What shall I do, o heart, o heart?
How shall I escape through a locked door?
He has smashed the furniture, my only defences,
And there is no refuge on the floor.

I HAVE NO DRUMS

I have no drums nor golden-throated bugles
But a reed pipe hollowed with my own hands
Which I keep in the attic in a small treasure-box
Locked carefully when I am not there.

I play it sometimes but the notes stumble,
Tripping in a jumble of fingers. My tense body
Cannot convey the meaning behind my eyes
To the tense air waiting, waiting

For the gold melody that long ago made the princes
Hack their way like men through the undergrowth of fear,
Bringing them to the valley where the sun shone strongly,
The crops flourished and the women of beauty lived.

And when I play, if my brother or sister hears
A few forlorn notes trailing disconsolately downstairs,
Screwing their eyes with pain and stuffing their ears,
They call resentfully to me to stop.

But I know that if I practise assiduously
I shall acquire the ten-fingered agility
To make the reed pipe describe like a camera
The vistas of my private pain.

Later, then, I shall buy not a trumpet but a clarinet
And, standing on a high hill, sound its keyed notes,
Making the warring armies look up in wonder
At me, forgetting their angry disputes.

SHADOWS

Among the tall heroes are none to understand
How the lightning terrifies and the thunder hurts,
How behind the appalling couch and the rigid high chairs
Devils crouch, snarling, waiting for their meal.

Locked in the cupboard on the top landing
For sure there are dragons rampant and terrible,
And what horrible gnomes, over and under the bed,
Menace the unconscious hours with their bald screeching.

Little boy, little boy, learn to be alone,
To grasp courage like straws and float on your fear
With the relaxed wariness of the swimmer, trained
To watch the threatening wave and the deceptive current,

For, in the banquet hall, at the gay reception,
Walking at night with your girl-friend or alone in your room,
You will have terror, like days, with you all the years of your life
And among the tall strangers, none will understand.

A PANE OF GLASS

The roadmenders outside my window sit all day
Hammering the paving stones to a definite shape
So that no fine lady or gallant gentleman should ignominiously
Be tripped or upset on the wet, dusty streets

And I all day behind my window with a pen
In my right hand sit and add up figures
Or write long, threatening letters to schoolteachers guilty
Of indiscretions really of no consequence.

A pane of glass divides the air between us, makes
Two worlds of one: a close examination will reveal
Flaws in the glass that, lingering on the cornea,
Distort for each the other's world and his own.

What but to break the glass and unhampered let me chip
My life to the required smooth even shape
And let the roadmender, if he so wishes, balance
The account of his days and threaten all the bosses.

NIGHT, AGAIN NIGHT

So still have I no rest from these barbed prongs
That mutter in the mind's high flesh and form:
The heart's sharp weapons that attack, deface
The curved sheer beauty of my reason's mould.

On my lips by day the laugh, the glittering
Worlds deploy, advance along the heart's terrain,
And all the snipers of sentimentality retreat
Before the mind's tough well-trained soldiery.

Yet at night by the dead light
Of the mind's unreason, traitorous friend,
The heart's battalions raise triumphant flags
And pitch their tents among my brain's tilled fields.

So do the castles of my delight kneel down,
The melancholy scavengers of fear come in
To brush the jagged grit of my happiness around
The eye-holes of my madness, my jerking head.

JULY EVENING — STORM COMING UP

On the water the accumulation of spume,
The hiss and purl of spiralling waves, the skid
And visible snarl of wind, horizon's disintegration,
The glower and sharp glint of a tired sky.

Nearer home, between my hand and the breaking water,
The inclination of leaves, the gnarled and aloof
Trunk of an old tree and, under my window,
The yellow disaster of forsythia. The first raindrops fall,
Papers disarray, curtains behave like flags.

Now for the decisions of night, the heart's undoing:
The time where reason and emotions meet.

THE CHOICE

It is too much for a man to be alone
All the time, equating laugh with moan,
Anger with joy, white sand with rigid stone,

Attempting to resolve a half-known equation,
Appraising the why and wherefore of his situation,
But always with the personal reservation.

That way madness lies. A tired Dean here
In Dublin, two centuries ago, year by year,
Heard approach the thunder and voiced his fear

Yet could not, though she waited to receive
Him eagerly with tenderness, make himself believe
Happiness as other than being well-deceived.

Reservations
1950

GIRL IN A RED DRESS

The bitch-eyed girl spoke to me warily
And more than a hand stirred my silk hair.
She had a red dress that was high-fashioned
By craftsmen glad of her casual favour

And low-tongued in exile were the virtuous ladies
Who had dangled their laughs at me with serious intention.
I spoke little to her, just answered her greeting,
Yet by night I knew that she was not a maid.

Now, though Heaven is witness that I did not wish it happen,
May the Lord retain me in the mood of this girl-eyed bitch
Who tears up my days and offers me no right compensation
For the stripped and spiked bone's-end of my mind she blunted.

WHITE, WHITE FLOWER

My flower was white and had beautiful petals,
A long, tough stalk, a green centre.
My mother gave it to me after breakfast,
Picking it specially in our own garden.

I walked in the streets with it, a shy hero,
Holding it in my left hand, a symbol of victory,
Knowing I had earned it but afraid of people
Looking, who would laugh at me for my simplicity.

They did not jeer but in their midst accepted me,
Me with my white flower and strange long fingers,
Me with my clumsy body and my peculiar slouch
And the awkwardness of nature in my eyes.

So I went to one that I thought loved me, thinking
She will like this flower my mother has given me,
And, taking it as a love-token, keep it
Later between a book's pages.

She was sitting in the window looking downstreet.
When she saw me, she burst out laughing.
Running towards me she took the flower and, laughing,
Tore it, breaking the beautiful petals.

DARK WAY

It is dark here and there are ghosts roving
Up and down among the trees and by the roadway.
Come closer, my darling, and let me guard you
From the evil that is round us and threatening.

These are the shapes of our wicked fancies
That, baulked in the daytime, gather round at night
With their terrible accusations and their gross demands,
Their exhortations and their meaning looks.

We recognise the things we never did,
Sins of omission, thoughtlessness that caused
Pain to others, the dross of our being
That, gathering behind the skin, now bursts outwards.

Come the morning redness of the day we'll find
These things have returned to their natural graves
Behind the blaséness of eyes and fingers,
The controlled nostrils and the firm mouth.

But we now, the big-eyed travellers, must forge ahead,
Prepared to meet these things each following night.
How can we figure out the blasé answers, having
No artificial daylight for the mind?

GULLS

The gulls bank back, daunted. Like a steamer
The wind destroys the sea's still even calm.
Under its monstrous caresses waves chop and menace
And we are aware of storm.
O gulls, gulls, brave ones, back like a parabola curve
In landwards home to your sheltered rock niches.
The morning glowers like an angry child but who can say
If anger will vanish at the sun's first sneaking kindness?
Later there will be time to think of the stress and strain
Of storm but now the safety of the cliff's face beckons.

So, too, my desires, arrowing birds
Native to my life's oceanic quietness,
Not daunted but with the instinct of self-protection
Before society's wrecking ill-natured storm-winds
Which tear and rip my natural morning's joy,
Swerve back to the mind's steep riddled cliff
To fret and fume in its gullies and black chasms.

SOLDIER FROM THE WARS

Somebody, I gather, is fishing in Galway,
In afternoon drift on the Corrib's lower reaches,
Hooking deftly the wet fish, returning
Easily to tea at sundown.

He is, I think, a young man with girls in his eyes —
Afternoon tennis and romantic late-night dances,
Hoping to meet later the gallant girl, marry,
Have two children, live comfortably in the country.

He has survived Dunkirk and the Grecian islands,
Coming unscathed to fight on the cliffs of Crete
And after in Africa, to and fro across the desert,
Seeking the promised land of his happiness.

And he has known also his private danger,
The ugly nip in the night from the crab-like claws
Of *Why didn't I do it* and *What should I say,*
Through the strait hours and no answer.

And now, eluding London and the swinging girls,
He comes to this backwater to attempt to hook
The five-foot-ten of happiness which is his birthright
Before his blood trumpets a more insidious war.

Whom I heard of casually in a Dublin bus, to this
Unknown young man my hand reaches, to answer
The wishes in his sinews and behind his eyes,
Unspoken in the gardens of his longing.

I pray that this unknown young man who has known
The lightning's strict hour, the time of anger
And the thunder within, may know also
The peace following always the days of action.

May he survive unscathed the Dunkirk of middle-age
And cardiac decay, the Crete of married life,
The Peloponnese-like archipelago of children, to fish lazily
In the reaches of a quiet old age.

THIS HOURE HER VIGILL

Elizabeth, frigidly stretched,
On a spring day surprised us
With her starched dignity and the quietness
Of her hands clasping a black cross.

With book and candle and holy water dish
She received us in the room with the blind down.
Her eyes were peculiarly closed and we knelt shyly
Noticing the blot of her hair on the white pillow.

We met that evening by the crumbling wall
In the field behind the house where I lived
And talked it over, but could find no reason
Why she had left us whom she had liked so much.

Death, yes, we understood: something to do
With age and decay, decrepit bodies;
But here was this vigorous one, aloof and prim,
Who would not answer our furtive whispers.

Next morning, hearing the priest call her name,
I fled outside, being full of certainty,
And cried my seven years against the church's stone wall.
For eighteen years I did not speak her name

Until this autumn day when, in a gale,
A sapling fell outside my window, its branches
Rebelliously blotting the lawn's green. Suddenly, I thought
Of Elizabeth, frigidly stretched.

NEW YEAR BELLS

Whether to bow a failure out
Or usher another failure in
The bells their murmurings begin
Is more than my pen can denote.

Perhaps this vile Dean, reeling round
The vestry in his night-shift,
Urging the mad bell-ringers sound,
Answers that each new year's gift
Is pain and strife and bursting heads?

But that was in another century;
And, of course, the man is dead.

CROSS GUNS BRIDGE

Once too often for my taste I shall cross
That bridge two miles north of Dublin where
On one side an orphanage, other, a gas-station,
Stand like twin guardian demons on this undoubting road.

Had they been chosen, what could be more appropriate
On the approach to a graveyard than these two buildings?
Some surrealist impulse welled up like spring-water
And tossed out this gas-station, this bridge and this orphanage.

There, opposite but more than similar, they stand, fit symbols:
One to remind the mourners how they all are homeless
Like the homeless one in the brass-bound coffin whom they follow
From the hub of life to the rim of clay-stopped quietness

And one to tell them how the days rush by,
The acceleration of seconds, the whining meanness of years,
How our minds run dry, how our lives start pinking,
How we need the hands of love to set them right again.

Not London Bridge of London Town but a decrepit structure
Spans the artificial river dividing city and cemetery,
Dividing dead and not-so-dead. It will collapse
Any day and a good many be caught unwittingly.

Yet who would anticipate evil in days like these
When it alights around us like birds unexpectedly
And steals through our chimneys and windows with the day
Of the light and the night of the dark as its cloaks.

Well to the south of Dublin, to-day I watch
The evening cloud over, the inclination of rain.
Outside my window, the green spume of the earth
Drenches the irises of my eyes and my girl is laughing.

ON SANDYMOUNT STRAND

These long years
Watching the seagulls bank and retreat daily
And the tide's remorseless flowing on the wrinkled
Forehead of the strand, I have been happy here,
Stealing apples from orchards and being chased,
Playing football and more mysterious games
Lost to me now, or breaking my heart
For a girl who broke her eight-year life she was so eager
To live and to experience everything well.

And there was poetry. When I found
Lines detonating in my mind and my pen
Stabbing the pages of my memory, I would have sold
My sister to the devil for a poem
Complete and lucid as spring-water, to startle
God and rock his golden throne.
It never came; yet I was happy, too,
With the snapping swords of words and the shields of tinsel phrases.

Gone, now, the adolescent swagger and closed
The book of my youth, ruled, and a trial
Balance extracted for my future use.
I thought to-day
As still the gulls banked and the evil tide
Crept nearer from the horizon while I walked
By Sandymount Tower, now decrepit and strewn
With rubble borne there by the wind and water,
How my youth wore down like an old shoe-sole
Sodden with age,

Leaving between me and the hostile, hard
Ground of society, nothing — nothing at all
Now to prevent the damp and the needling chill
Eating into my bones and burrowing to my heart.

UNDERWORLD

Under this stone, flat, grey, undistinguished
From any other stone in this desolate village
Among the green decay, remnant of a proud
Fall of rain, descant of spring, clear aria
Of water faltering on frond of valley, falling,

There is an urgency of movement, unexpected
Like the blunt stab of sunlight into a dark room,
And where in the sunray from darkness is seen
The world of dust, its frightening industry,
The silence and the swiftness of its menace,

So, under this familiar stone, the unguessed movements,
The reeling zigzags, the back-and-forward dartings
Importune our understanding, our stunned concern.
Something terrible is here we had not dreamt of,
We had not allowed for in our calculations:

The hungry importance of life is precise here beneath
The veneer of decay, the riotousness of moss — a tailpiece
Of truth, a scut of beauty.
                                              Lay back the stone.
It is late for walking these savage lanes.
Something unknown is doing something unknowable,
Building, perhaps, a better poor world for its progeny.

DIRGE FOR THE LIVING SELF

Iron and sticks to cover my bones,
Money for drinks and a murmuring priest –
Why won't they let me rest in peace?

Where is the girl-eyed boy I loved
Whose hair I tossed with shy intention
And never made him my confession?

Six years down with fingers cramped
He busies himself with tubers and weeds
And roots spat out by unknown seeds.

O dead man, to kiss you now
I rip the skies and strip the earth
And join in everybody's mirth

But when the glass is at my lips
And when my true love gaily cries
Your knuckles iron out my eyes.

SONG

I bring you laughs and keep the tears myself
As I walk to you across the night
Who are the rich orchard of my delight,
My fount of happiness, my wishing well

And all the pears of your aloofness fall
To gabble in these hot gardens like bursting children
Who glimpsed the daring of the witches' cauldron
And to their own burning gave no thought at all.

Love, I have wandered like a blinded Jew,
And now, over the night, my promised land,
You wait for me, kiss in hand,
As lithely I step the remaining miles to you

Who can pin the winds like any insolent Spaniard
Or pierce the tide's malignant eye
With the needle of your happiness and joy.
So, while to-night you are the fine vanguard

To cut the yellow harvest of my years
That flowers in the valley
Of my stony agony,
I bring you laughs; I store away the tears.

STONY SOIL

Locked under the clay the seed uncoils
Slowly, in late spring, under a fair sun,
The first efforts at roots, the shy tendrils touching
The unembarrassed earth, softly, oh! gently,
With April tentative music of finch and blackbird.

And later under the sun's outspoken encouragement,
With youth's fine confidence these growing roots
Grip and twine round and hug the yielding soil,
Bolder the advances, rougher the caresses.
The denial of winter will soon be made good:

Autumn shall see the final vehemence
Of seed and soil shocked in their last embrace,
The male arrogance of corn, the pulsing,
Singing sap in root and drunken flower,
The sensuous triumph, the acclamation of leaves.

But here is stony soil: my life's short roots
Snap and break off in society's tough earth.
So spring and winter are the same to me
Whose seed is stunted with the year's advance.
I have no hands to mutter how I cry
Or love to guard the tendrils of my days.

GOOD-TIME GIRL

'No,' she said, 'Why should I? I don't want
To settle down. I'm only twenty-three.
I've got a dream of ribbons in my hair
And dances at the cross-roads, gay and free.

Him? Oh, he understands. He knows a girl
Must stagger out a verse to make a rhyme.'
I thought of Empson and Anita Loos:
A girl can't keep on laughing all the time.

Someone should tell her how the years drip down
Like water from a leaking cistern, wearing out
The patience of the best; and how the silver
Mirror gives no occasion for regret.

THE DOG

All day the unnatural barking of dogs
Sounded in my ears. In O'Connell Street, among the crowds,
A dog barked at my heels but, when I looked, was gone.
Sitting at my window, later, at nearly three o'clock,
Glad for the quiet harmony of the afternoon,
A voice reached up like a long arm out of the street
To rap on the shutters of my ears but, when I looked,
The street's chaste line was unbroken, its perspective unstrained.

Now, lying awake in bed, smoking,
Looking out the window, I can see him,
Lean-faced and shaggy, as the moonlight falls
Sideways into my room as into a chapel,
Where he squats on the lawn and tilts his lonely snout,
Raising his lost unnatural cry.

God send his master is not dead or none he loves,
Being out of countenance, has sent him for succour
And that I don't understand his plaintiveness:
But yet, God help me, I fear this unnatural barking
Has something to do with me and not with strangers,
As quietly I lie, hearing the hours tick by,
And the unsatisfied dog, howling upon the lawn,
Breaking the night's maidenhead.

SPRING JAG
for Avril Webb, 1944.

Spring stops me suddenly like ground
Glass under a door, squeaking and gibbering.
I put my hand to my cheek and the tips
Of my fingers feel blood pulsing and quivering.

A bud on a branch brushes the back
Of my hand and I look, without moving, down.
Summer is there, screwed and fused, compressed,
Neat as a bomb, its casing a dull brown.

From the window of a farther tree I hear
A chirp and a twitter: I blink.
A tow-headed vamp of a finch on a branch
Cocks a roving eye, tips me the wink

And, instantly, the whole great hot-lipped ensemble
Of buds and birds, of clay and glass doors,
Reels in with its ragtime chorus, staggering
The theme of the time, a jam-session's rattle and roar,

With drums of summer jittering in the background
Dully and, deeper down and more human, the sobbing
Oboes of autumn falling across the track of the tune,
Winter's furtive bassoon like a sea-lion snorting and bobbing.

There is something here I do not get,
Some menace that I do not comprehend
Yet so intoxicating is the song
I cannot follow its thought right to the end.

So up the garden path I go with spring
Promising sacks and robes to rig my years
And a young girl to gladden my heart in a tartan
Scarf and freedom from my facile fears.

SPRING STOMP

Now while the early sun
Smears the fields with morning,
I will ask my love to come
Trucking down the dawn,
As spring's advance live agents
Of buds and migrant birds
Herald a summer coming
Like thunder from the south.

O love, when we suffer under
Our autumn's cruel regime,
What laws can quell the rebel
Armies of memory,
Or stop the broken lines
Of poems streeling through
The wasted fields of our
Imagination's farms?

So, love, let you come dancing
Down the jazzy lanes of spring,
Through the ragtime green of meadows
By the high cliff's muted brink.
Let's swing it by the river
To the torch-song of the water
While yet our sinews answer
The off-beat's hot-licked pause.

RESERVATIONS

'Twenty crocuses in my garden to-day', she said,
'I know spring is here.' She lay on the bed,
Happily, while I stood at the window, sideways,
Thinking, 'This is how it has been always.

Somebody else has been happy because spring was here,
Lazily turning on a bed, smiling. The mere
Veneer of acquiescence was all I ever possessed.'
I know there is a lot that I have missed

Yet, afraid of March gales, there was nothing I could do
But agree, with reservations — remembering, too,
How winter struck us dumb, not so long ago,
And how it would pay us back for spring, blow for blow.

DESCENDING

I'm going down,' she said, tying her yellow scarf,
While I still watched the dull grey mountain road
Mooch down into the glen and disappear
Round a curve of trees and cottages. Some sudden fear
Made me not reply or make any attempt to start
Yet awhile; I sat on the old sacrificial stone

To which we had climbed all the hot morning together,
Choosing the difficult way, along the dried-up river bed
Choked with dead boulders covered with a fur of spruce leaves.
Not even the sacrifice of our youth — made at noon — redeems
The swinging boughs of our minds, gay with feathers,
Lopped from us now. I'm going down,' she said.

Her teeth were hedges of dense, white sloe-blossom,
Her hair a development of black. Down the afternoon
From the rare peak of youth, too, we are going, to the valley
Of age, lurching and stumbling down its gothic alleys
And grotesque approaches. 'I'm going down.' The gossip
Of the wind in her hair will be stopped much too soon.

A MARRIAGE HAS BEEN ARRANGED

'Yes,' she said, 'I am happy,' turning the ring
On her finger three times for luck. Spring
Outside the window, ticked off winter who was beyond retorting.
The curtains blew inwards and upwards softly
As she stood, gazing at something I could not see
Far beyond the small pond and the crooked walnut tree.

I was glad for her but could not restrain
A thread of sorrow being pulled through my brain.
How she would marry and decay into contentment
Occasioned in me some amount of resentment
Against the ways and means of our emotional lives,
Their sharp and cunningly concealed knives.

The problem, of course, is to hold this minute Now
In perpetuo while growing ourselves to ripeness; how
To have Time held up by some blunt traffic cop
So letting us, the unfortunate pedestrians, across.
It can't be done, I suppose; so I wish her, my dear,
As much happiness as she can conveniently bear.

THE GULL

Some bitch of a bird yelled dog's abuse
At me this morning when I woke up.
Flat on my back I listened, stunned
By the bad-tempered tirade that never stopped

Once even for breath or to choose a word.
From her tongue's tip a sailor's range
Of invective, blue as the sky, spearing towards me
Slewed and ricochetted against the window pane,

As she made her own of the five-tone scale
With a design of grace-notes no coal-quay shawlie
Could shuffle together on a sunny morning
Or drunk in a pub in an evening's brawling.

This was what I had feared all along;
Trick-o-the-loop Nature, street-angel, house-devil.
Well I guessed the sheen on the far green hills
To be the smooth evil of satin, its moral level.

So, while at the window, a wicked bird frantically
Crumpled the morning tissue of silence, I resolved
To put as much distance between Nature's red claws
And myself as the years could make possible.

For me the Queensberry game, the built-up manner, the artificial,
Will be some vantage-point from which to view the wild,
Afford delaying actions while I make some judgements
Uninfluenced by the terror of a child,

And, in due course, questioned, I'll reply
That the great white bird with the cruel beak was to blame
Who, one sunny quiet morning in May, suddenly frightened me,
Roaring, cursing and spitting against the window-pane.

ELEGY FOR THE COMMENCEMENT OF WINTER

These apple trees shall be resplendent again
In their pearl-draped vanity, when summer smacks hard
Home in the next year, playing its trump card
After winter's gamble and the spring's slick stratagem.
These bushes, too, the berry and the currant,
Shall swank it through the autumn in their new rig-out,
Swaying their laden shoulders with the seductive, insolent
Assurance of girls in evening dress dining out.

Who would have the heart to speak then of decline?
Not I, nor Elizabeth; although each new summer
For us is not a period of festival, of drumming
Blood flowering and shooting a line
But another warped and rusted leaf to cover
The rich earth of our youth and our horn-mad days
When every note of the clock brought us another lover
Each, and another love-song to phrase.

Now while winter strikes its first-round gong
Bringing all the dryads, crying, from the woods,
If you look carefully, you will see the buds
Curled up snugly in their own warmth.
Already they plan dresses, make their dates, decide
The menus for their roaring parties, engage
The bands that will provide both sweet and jive
When light-fingered spring flicks over another page.

But from me, in this garden, confidence slips like a shawl,
Watching the leaves like damaged gliders toss
And tailspin in the southern warm wind and cut across
The path, between her and the low granite wall,
Knowing the infective evil latent
In their rust, how the disease, contracted, spreads,
The limbs, once cramped, never to be again straightened
Or summer detonate in our heads.

BY THE DODDER IN FLOOD AT HERBERT BRIDGE

In this river, flooded by recent rains,
The current sobs heavily like a girl
Watching her day angrily warp and curl
Into scales of white foam like a dragon's mail.
Danger is on tap like oil, insolent, yet all
The olive-green pike, the brilliant-finned perch, behind the wall
Of weeds, where the shallows were, can cower
Grimly, counting their safety out hour by hour.

Looking across the garden towards the river, alone, I think
How for us, flooded by circumstances, no weedy margins
Offer their dubious protection, as we stand, uncertain,
With our hands hanging, by winter's brink,
Yet ours, all spring and summer, was the shrewd concentration
On crops and fuel, preparing for this evil season,
Neither flowers nor birds tempting our attention nor even
Gay girls laughing in the hay-meadows, wheedling.

Silently, in late November, we in this soured land
Wait the Hunger Moon, the days closing in, rain
Gunning the windows, the wind rising, the pain
Of winter already in our numbed hands.
How will we live for the next twelve months
Is the bare question, seeing the results
Of our year's labour, turf-clamps ruined, the tempting
Harvest lost and all our store-houses empty.

THE COMING DAY

'Every man has his price.' The cyclist rode by
His comment to his comrade on the rackets
Of politics and business nuzzling in my ears.
I walked steadily on, hands in dustcoat pockets,
Knowing that, no matter how much I tried,
I could not stop the thought that slipped and veered

By the foreshore of my mind like a water-wag
Disturbing the calm of my sleep for nights to come
Or tilting the horizon-line of my day and age.
Suppose that for some guarantee of peace and ease, or some
Other form of happiness, my now taut ideals sag
Letting my life absorb the shocks of joy and rage,

What then? What, indeed, then. I do not know.
To-day my left hand is on my desk and the sun shines on
The long curious fingers that people admire. It is early
To be regretting the things that will be gone,
The fine-drawn skin, the midday sun, the hot ideals that show
Indulgence, lack of integrity or false sympathy rarely.

Yet now, in my twenty-sixth year, the questions are being written
    down
And the day upon which I must reply draws near.
I have no answers ready; so I am not much surprised
That every sentence strips some nerve of fear,
Or that, walking in streets or sitting in rooms, the sound
Of voices frightens me, their menace being so thinly disguised.

CLEAR VIEW IN SUMMER

Heavy with leaves the garden bushes again
Sun, and the trees admire them, lazily.
Cabbages and carnations, drills and beds of them, droop tiredly
And far away the hills, like dry dogs, crouching, squeal for water.
Love, who is it whispers everything is in order
On this summer afternoon, when nothing moves, not even the flies,
    strangely,
As we relax by the lawn, here under the pear-tree, watching idly
The leaves declining, the shadows surely lengthen.

But it won't be always summer — not for us; there are bad times
    coming
When you and I will look with envy on old photographs,
Remembering how we stood, there in the sun, looking like gods,
While the days of our lives, like fruit, swelled and decayed,
And how, by the lake,
Its surface, one August evening, unchipped, walking, we laughed
As Love slipped his arms through ours and we gladly followed
The path he showed us through life's valley running.

There'll be much to recall then, when, like wet late summer leaves,
The days under our tread don't rustle, no other summer waiting
Around the turn of a new year with rich clothes to grace us
Whose subtle beauty will have long since languished;
And Nature's flashing greenness will stitch up our hearts with
    anguish
Each day when August with sunlight riddles the branches, the leaves
    taking
Voluptuously the south west wind's caresses
Year after dying year.

And yet the declension of each following season, each day's
Defection, splits open our hope only and not our courage, safe and
   sound
In the deep shelter of our awareness; the bushes and tall trees
Flourish and go down unconsciously in defeat
While full-grown man, whose pride the angels weep,
Watches love itself gutter out some dull evening, nobody around,
Winter moving in, no fuel left, the lights not working, the lease
Unrenewable, summer a seldom-remembered scat-phrase.

MIRAGE

They had the blind and beautiful eyes of statues
But their bodies had vitality, were eager to be loved,
And all were graceful with a suggestion of swallows.
Since sometimes, then, there seems no end to love
(The night has its own devices and even the day
A trick or two to delude the unwary heart,
Make yearn the fingers, the blood long, the body tentatively
    shudder)

Why shouldn't the heart, sick with loneliness,
Turn to them naturally as the needle, swinging, turns north
Home to the ice-lidded, lifeless desert covering
The burning magnetic centre of its love,
Wish for warmth in these sodden days, dripping
With fear, hope dirty in the gutters, the horizon of grief
Dragging the road away always, the sinews rotting?

Yet it was heart-breaking, waking to a bright morning
In autumn, watching through the window the leaves take off
In a west wind, turning, to see those eyes, blank, uncomprehending,
And, a gull's harsh voice slithering down your ear-drum,
Know where the truth lay, that you were lonelier than trees
Stripped in winter, no summer consolation of fruition
Yours, not even the spring expectancy.

HECTOR

Talking to her, he knew it was the end,
The last time he'd speed her into sleep with kisses:
Achilles had it in for him and was fighting mad.
The roads of his longing she again wandered,
A girl desirable as midsummer's day.

He was a marked man and he knew it,
Being no match for Achilles whom the gods were backing.
Sadly he spoke to her for hours, his heart
Snapping like sticks, she on his shoulder crying.
Yet, sorry only that the meaning eluded him,

He slept well all night, having caressed
Andromache like a flower, though in a dream he saw
A body lying on the sands, huddled and bleeding,
Near the feet a sword in bits and by the head
An upturned, dented helmet.

FROM NEW ROSS

In this quiet town it is odd to discover
A day buried so deeply in the debris of years
And to dig it out, not damaged at all, discoloured
With dust to be wiped away like tears.
Why here of all places? Was it the fall
Of sunlight on the trees beyond, or the startling call
Of a trumpet unexpectedly down the street, lay
Flush with the memory and pathos of that day?

Say, anyhow, it was: for love like trumpets then
Shattered the walls of our reserve in a sunlit garden
When, over the hedge, you threw the cherries to me and again
Innocence gave us a blessing and a pardon
As little we thought of the fleet, disturbing swallow
Along air-lanes in the garden skidding, stuttering its warning
Of night over the horizon implacably throbbing
With answers both for our laughing and our sobbing.

O Elizabeth, the gold trumpets no more
Curl for you their notes, though the cherry-tree
Each year displays its wares in hope
Your fingers will fondle them caressingly,
And here is my youth, like a bright ribbon, soiled
By death, my days, the dustbin gang, the broken delph, destroyed
By hopes that leave like visitors and leave
A trail of stains that smiling won't conceal.

Yet now, watching the swallows bank over the trees
There where the river bends, suddenly I find time to wonder
What can stop the cough in my life or ease
The choking effects of so many blunders —
Somewhere there should be love aloud like music.
Over the hunching hills, the wires go trailing their furious
Messages, the oiled machinery of nature shunts
Day down for repairs. Silently the night's technicians hunt.

ICARUS

As, even to-day, the airman, feeling the plane sweat
Suddenly, seeing the horizon tilt up gravely, the wings shiver,
Knows that, for once, Daedalus has slipped up badly
Drunk on the job, perhaps, more likely dreaming, high-flier Icarus,
Head butting down, skidding along the light-shafts
Back, over the tones of the sea-waves and the slip-stream, heard
The gravel-voiced, stuttering trumpets of his heart

Sennet among the crumbling court-yards of his brain the mistake
Of trusting somebody else on an important affair like this;
And, while the flat sea, approaching, buckled into oh! avenues
Of acclamation, he saw the wrong story fan out into history,
Truth, undefined, lost in his own neglect. On the hills,
The summer-shackled hills, the sun spanged all day;
Love and the world were young and there was no ending:

But star-chaser, big-time-going, chancer Icarus
Like a dog on the sea lay and the girls forgot him,
And Daedalus, too busy hammering another job,
Remembered him only in pubs. No bugler at all
Sobbed taps for the young fool then, reported missing,
Presumed drowned, wing-bones and feathers on the tides
Drifting in casually, one by one.

LACKENDARRAGH
I.M. my friend the poet Bill Clare, d. by drowning 1942

And it was summer the day — late as usual, the middle
Of August, I think — and I thought how, then, little
    If any should die on a red evening
And hollow-chested Maulin and big-dugged Old Boleys pinned up
    That Sunday right then for me,
        Wishing me more luck
Any day. O it was sweet in the valley gleaming
    With girls to go taunting
And thwarting the evening that night and the next season,
All over the shoulders of Boleys warily peeping.

And lucky was I, knew I it, to cradle my arms round
A sunray at six, in my twenty-first year on the ground,
    The days going down like armies;
But the river was talking fast, you were laughing, I couldn't be
        bothered
    Thinking how later I'd like to remember
    Odd sunrays like gossip.
Had later been mentioned, I'd only have said, 'What harm is
    It, laughing like this, though September
Be down round the corner?' We were young, we were gay
And rich in the worship of a simple day.

O younger than summer easily, the apple-hung and the berry-
        studded
Days dropping ripe into our hands, walking the wooded
    Inclines of the valley, we had nothing
To do with death, although around us already, being August, the
        candles

Of autumn flared out one by one
And summer her bangles
Her jewels, her castanets and daring dresses was putting
Away sorrowfully: all being done
With; we were the last romantics there and then, flaunting
Our hearts asleeve, by the log-bridged river ranting.

Still on the air, though than I older far, the river
Unscripted larks, dayfree now as then, never
The poor mouth on or a grumble;
But down in the valley this later August grieves,
I see, the green exotic summer,
A revelry of leaves
Frittering out ineptly; and I, hearing the black tick in the year,
wonder
When was our tuppeny-coloured
World: the river talks fast but I can't answer,
Knowing now each minute the last one cancels

— Knowing Time, that brings the leaf to book but leaves
A river gabble away a good Sunday any year,
For winter, the old wound, probes
In the heel of this season. Bleakly the bluff I essay,
Hoping defeat has its pride
Whatever it may
Be: for love will be missing in the latter end, an old
Shoe worn out and cast by,
Left rotting on some forgotten road long before and far away
Over the hills on a perhaps like this religious day.

TIME, THE FAITHLESS

All evening, while the summer trees were crying
Their sudden realisation of the spring's sad death,
Somewhere a clock was ticking and we heard it here
In the sun-porch, where we sat so long, buying
Thoughts for a penny from each other. Near
Enough it was and loud to make us talk beneath our breath.

And a time for quiet talking it was, to be sure, although
The rain would have drowned the sound of our combined voices.
The spring of our youth that night suddenly died
And summer filled the veins of our lives like slow
Water into creeks edging. Like the trees you cried.
Autumn and winter, you said, had so many disguises

And how could we be always on the watch to plot
A true perspective for each minute's value? I couldn't reply,
So many of my days toppled into the past, unnoticed.
Silence like sorrow multiplied around you, a lot
Of whose days counted so much. My heart revolted
That time for you should be such a treacherous ally

And though, midnight inclining bells over the city
With a shower of sound like tambourines of Spain
Gay in the teeth of the night air, I thought
Of a man who said the truth was in the pity,
Somehow, under the night's punched curtain, I was lost.
I only knew the pity and the pain.

POEM IN THE DEPTHS OF SUMMER
for Sheila

Here, now, again, in this garden, I watch the summer
  Burn away, June alight,
The season's torch crackling: and O among the flowers,
  My childhood drumming
  On my memory, nights
And days of red-faced vigour I remember when the hours,
Each one of them a long lane, faced me and, brave
  Child I, I essayed them unafraid.

Gripped in my fist the burning season then each hour's
  Holes and corners lit
Up brightly and slyly I hid myself, chuckling with joy;
  And the roistering flowers
  Through the slits
Of their lives, hopped out and searched for me, a boy
Free as air evading them, shouting and laughing and running
  Round each day's turning.

Lost long since, those days: but, girl, you, who came
  To me with the good
Weather this year, the lamb and the crocus, the birds,
  Have suddenly made
  Them again real. Could
Summer have presented me flowers topping you with your words
  Of joy, laughing among the hours, calling to me gaily
Love is never failing?

Summer flickers down, I know; but, my darling, we
  Have something on tap
To tide us from year to year: a reserve of love
  Deep and free;
  And, though winter, perhaps,
Invest us, here we have sustenance, over and above
Our possible needs — till like trees we blossom
  Again, our lives' leaves tossing.

Horan's Field
and Other
Reservations

1972

THE INVOCATION

Ten bloody years with this quill lying
Almost idle on my table, I have sourly watched

The narrow summers go, the winters ride over,
Awaiting always, seized in a cold silence,

The genetic word, the arrogant vaticinal line.
And each spring, unmoving by an open window,

The room ringing with emptiness like an unswung bell,
My noteboook open, filled with abstract questions,

The bare trees outside expectant, I saw the crocus tell
The indolent fall of the autumn leaves, another year's

Bitter burning and the ice again forming.

Lie with me now, therefore, these wording days,
The ever-questing, tragic-gesturing mind this spring exulting,

Lady I have icily waited for, whom I have known
By these aboding mountains, this lovely glen.

FOR A GIRL ON HER TWENTY-FIRST BIRTHDAY WHOSE PARTY I MISSED

Greetings

Much that you have hitherto learned must be re-examined in the light of a mature mind. And those things, unknown as yet, which will lie in your path must be approached with more circumspection than was your wont when, as an infant, you sported in the sun and made light of the death-agonies of worms. Those who have little virtue to recommend them to civil gentry must be shunned as the abomination or the mouse; for the inhabitants of this island are prone to indolence, yea, sloth, drunkenness and other idle graces.

Apply yourself to your studies, Avril Webb.

SWEENEY'S SHORT SONG COME CANDLEMAS

O lucky the lad whose lass can lilt
A summery song this winter weather
When the ice lies over the loach lake
And the berry dies on the holly bush.

Not dull the day that with delight
The lass can carol her crony home
Though the dunlin keels on its brown back
And the frost nobbles the jenny wren.

FRAGMENT FROM AN UNFINISHED POEM

    Now not any more of summer
This year, its light so golden, all shining, ducking down
    The reaches of the valley, the leaf-ridden lanes
    Of my heart, too, with its gold-looking joy
    Stippled and the brown
Earth, like a girl, sung in its warmth, I should think, so
    Swiftly its din to a murmur
Falls this morning. Rising, I wait for Autumn, as strains
Of Summer's music while up the garden, unhappy again, I go,
    Down the avenues of daylight die.

    Into the morning siphons
Surely the doom all August, the great-clappered honeysuckle
    Clanging down the valley, we denied:
    Slowly, leaf after leaf loosing, calmly,
    Summer so subtly
Its strategic withdrawal devises and Autumn, over these sun-loving
        broad
    Acres, melancholy, frightening, silent
Invader, is beamed in gradually; and again, as ever, with a child's
Unease and indecision, I watch, this gloomy Sunday, sloping off,
    The lovely sun's green armies.

THE OLD HOUSE

Simply to come to it again, having been absent
For many years — marriage, children, the tiring
Duties of provision: things in a dubious world
Themselves worthy enough.

Often he wondered whether the new wing he added
Shortly before he left had a sure foundation,
A good dampcourse; and whether the timber, carefully fitted,
Had been sufficiently seasoned.

Looking at it now from the roadway, it seems to stand
Solidly against the main building, not too brash, ageing
In a dignified reticence as the evening cool sun
Slants over the hill just westward

And along the drive, slowly, as becomes a prodigal
Knowing the family, curious, detached, watching,
Heir now to the whole house and its rich broad acres,
He moves towards possession.

I. M. EDITH McFADDEN
d. aet. 24, 27 June 1950

Littler than I, she has gone on
Brashly into darkness, a slip of a girl.
With her fingers crossed, she scorned
Waiting any longer.

Grey-whiskered Death, our renowned daddy, deployer of all,
Alone knows where she now goes; the gardens fruitlessly echo
To the name of her name, the wind in the trees
Ceaselessly vowelling it . . .

Chider of angels, your humble servant,
Kneeling, discreetly distant, meticulously asking,
This bleak midsummer day, for this lost girl,
That famous mercy, the sward outside
In its order receptively disturbed, the broken
Vase of her laughter scattered across it carelessly.

FOOTNOTE TO MARXISM
for Christine, 1952

He liked to play games with his children ....
Edmund Wilson: *To the Finland Station.*

The bucking children on the sitting room floor,
The scattered toys, the dog-eared children's books,
The furniture shoved in any convenient nook,
The table on its end against the door
Draped in a grey camping blanket as a kind
Of hide-out, staff headquarters or simple eating-joint
(The purpose varying with demands of action, the points
For decision or the stolid needs of time)

— This Marx-like setting shows us a roughly honest world
Where shades of meaning, subtle and clever phrasing
Such as concern the scholar who owns the table
Are uncalled for. The logical accurate words
That spang around the room convey the exact sense
They are meant to, in a strictly present tense.

JANE BROWNE

Jane Browne had red hair that dazzled
The boys in Sandymount when she was even eight.
Going from school, all would be eager
Politely to see her to the garden gate

And, anxious to please, until she reached the door
Where she turned on the step and waved goodbye,
They waited; as ten years later they waited
Patiently on her with love-struck sighs.

Each was delighted with her merest favour,
Missing the mockery in her modest eyes
As she bent for a light or her mischievous laughter
Tinkled in the moony sky.

God love you, Miss Jane Browne. I had forgotten
Your pale cheeks, your smile, your red hair,
Our walks by Marlay, our melancholy love-glances,
Our kiss on the darkened stair . . .

And I would have had it like that; for when someone today
Said you died during a bitter war in pain,
Twenty years crashed down around me like gravel
And suddenly the garden daffodils were bursting around you again

As over your gate in married middle age
Memory leaned in grief. The reflecting mind
Marked off not empty minutes but those years
Of silence by your absence now defined.

THE EVE OF DESTRUCTION
for Suds and Gibbles

One daffodil
So brilliantly yellow,
Its head hanging over
On a piece of waste ground
In this cruel arctic April.

Two cosmonauts
In space now.
Let's pretend, darlings,
We don't know
What they're doing.

Marginalia these words, maybe,
Such as the old wise
Monks left us.

For the record, then,
If it survives,
I'm sorry our grandchildren
Won't be able even to

See

Such a yellow Daffodil.

THE MASTER PLAN

In the beginning
You lie on your back,
Eyes closed,
Arms tentatively moving,
An occasional cry.

Later, tossing and turning
For many years,
You wonder at the apparently
Haphazard movements of life,
Of nature, of joys,
Of griefs, humiliations,
Of memories too many to count.

In the end
You lie on your back,
Eyes closed,
Arms over chest stilled,
No cry at all.

DUE TO A TECHNICAL FAULT

Three days gone now
And no letters.

They've stopped delivery because
It doesn't matter any more

To them or to
Us.

Communication is through.

I don't know what's happening
Do you?

Over there in Mount Pleasant
They're counting sacks of mail

Not, of course
For you
Or me.

What a life of idle grace
They're having.

Tomorrow
Will be the fourth day.

Will anything happen

Tonight?

SANDYMOUNT NOW
for Frank Biggar

No one should go
Back to the old places.
Too many one knew
Are dead,
Old slow remembered customs
Gone with them.

And the streets, besides,
Seem narrower
In any event.
The Green tidied up
By the Municipal Council,
The rough fields covered
By semi-detacheds
With tiny gardens,
The teeming tumultuous sea
Pushed further back
By a new wall;
All disturbing elements
Pretty nearly
Accounted for

— Including, alas,
Regret,
Which, at any time,
Is irrelevant.

BEFORE THE END

Just keep on saying
No.

Tape it and attach
The tape to the telephone
To save your breath:
Slag down to the boozer
For what may be positively, definitely,
(You know how these things are)
Your Final Appearance
And your last drink.

Every time you're asked
To fill up a form
Scribble the word down twice

— In the margin always.

Not all that good, daughter,
In the latter end for you

— Speaking personally
I mean
You.

I, of course,
Am mooching off
Down to World's End
For a drink.
They're after me, too.

The writing is on the wall
In blood this time
Some of it yours, some mine,

Daughter.

ON SOME BOILER
at the Delhi Station

The vulture on the tree in the garden,
A close eye on the six labrador pups;

The mynah bird, strutting, preening and squealing,
My younger daughters strutting, preening and squealing;

John Montague, a bullying friend in Paris, worried,
Me in New Delhi, worried;

Kevin Nowlan, a professional historian,
Addressing a demo from a balcony

In a worthy cause;
Roger McHugh in the lotus position this minute

Staring at an oval-faced geisha girl, and explaining
The philosophical nature of Noh;

Martin Sheridan, reverentially excoriating
In the name of the Lord, *la condition humaine;*

Harry Boylan, saturnine in a sailing boat,
Some obscure gaelic saying on his lips as the mast breaks;

Conor Cruise O'Brien, a Voltaire cultivating his garden
At Whitewater where we were all so happy

Sometime; across the bay, lovely Sandymount
Where we were all so happy sometime;

The thunder breaks now in Delhi: Montague arrives
Again, as ever, a Northern chip on his shoulder

And breaking old moulds.

These friends:
Intelligible realities — the food for contemplation.

HORAN'S FIELD

In torn ganseys, patched worsted pants, we played
Seven-a-side rugby in winter there.
We had no goal-posts — a few ganseys
Pulled off as we warmed up
Did to make goal at each end of the pitch.
Touch was if the ball hit
The back walls of the houses
Fifty yards off on one side. On the other side,
Touch was where the ball was canted
Into the plots where needy people,
Like our parents, were allocated
Patches of ground to grow vegetables in
— Cheaper than shop-buying.

The field was owned by Mr. Horan, the butcher
— Blue pinafore, blue and white striped apron,
A cleaver, meat-saw or meat-knife
Perpetually in his hand as he hacked
Hunks of steak from cow, sheep, calf
Carcases hanging behind him, his hands
Red with liver-blood (a favourite
Delicacy in Sandymount —
Liver, I mean, not blood).
A decent man, Mr. Horan, who died,
As we all do, too soon.

Monkstown Third Fifteen
Played there every Saturday.
We were proud to call ourselves
Monkstown Fourths — without authority
Of any kind save the normal human
Desire for aggrandisement.
I played fly-half and Tommy
Scrum-half. Ball under my arm,
Rushing for the goal-line,
Like the Gaels going forth to battle,
I always fell. Being tackled invariably
By Louis was like being run
Down by a medium-sized tank.
I never scored, not once.

On the houses' side of the field
Was waste ground — moundy, scutch-grassed,
Overlaid here and there with
Cast out sheets of corrugated tin,
Rusty, holed and easy to cut yourself on.
Skeletons of what once had been
Prams holding the family pride,
Bits of old car doors,
— We used these to make dug-outs
For our serious gang-warfare with other
Boys from the village even more
Tattered and torn than we were.

At one end of this waste ground
Was a wall which we frequently climbed
And sat astride to admire
A formal garden such as we knew
We would never have — roses, tulips, sweetpea,
Daffodils, gladioli, chrysanthemums
(Whatever was in season),
Apple trees, goosegob, raspberry, strawberry bushes
— All the delights of envious childhood.
We sat there until the owner came
And ordered us down. It was a constant
Amazement to us such a garden's owner
Should dispense
Porter in the dirtiest pub in the village.

There was another house, barrack-like,
With nothing in the garden
Save the well-kept lawn
And a few trees.
Over the wall we gazed
In horrified fascination at the house,
Garden and out-houses. It was
An experimental Veterinary Station.
We knew the owner had hundreds
Of white rabbits locked up in cages
In the outhouses for some diabolical
Purposes.
We could hear the rabbits squealing.
We shared their locked-up agony,
We shared it and vowed
Retributive vengeance sometime.
In the meantime, we stole the vet's apples.

It was not, however, all pains, aches
And agony. I had a twelve-year-old's love
For tubby, tousle-headed, red-haired Marise
(Tommy preferred sloe-eyed, raven-haired Betty).
Lying there in the field at the end
Nearest the strand — only a one-foot,
Broken-down wall behind us —
We relaxed holding innocent hands.
Flat on our backs, she pretty in her
Blue tailored gym-slip, me caked in mud
From the hour-long game, we gazed
Straight up at the clear blue sky
(I cannot recall rain, fog or cloudy skies
In those astonishing days).
In time, to avoid parental trouble,
We went home to do our homework.
At six o'clock the day was over

Where are Marise and Betty now?
Sean, Pudgy, Builder, Ledser,
Kitty, Celia, Margaret, Finn,
Fisher, Luger, Mooner, Eve?
The girls, I suppose, are married,
The boys too, and stuck half-way
Through a desk like myself.
We were famous people in our day
And to all and to the boy
I feel now holding this pen,
I send my reminiscent love.
Marise, Marise, the world is at us all.
It falls upon us like a Himalayan peak
And we are trapped, no hope at all,

The rope broken, the crampons gone.
Above, above, a persuasive sky
But now no way back for homework.
Marise, Marise, the best is yet to be,
We're told — that solemn grown-ups' fantasy.
We boxed on the waste ground too,
An elimination contest every quarter.
I wasn't much good but once,
By staying out of punishment's way,
Running backwards to a hump in the ground
Where I knew I could fall accidentally, convincingly,
I managed to collect enough points,
In avoiding Pudgy's flailing fists,
To get me to the quarter final.
The two best fighters were Pudgy
And Butcher Boy (he wore butcher-blue suits).
Butcher Boy ran away from home at fourteen
Because his mother beat him regularly
Every day for his own good; and he couldn't hit back.
He joined the British Army,
Is believed killed in the last war.

Horan's field is gone now, a mass
Of handkerchief-lawned semi-detacheds
Covers it
This thirty-five years.
The one-foot broken wall,
The sandy mounds that faced the sea's dark
Winter anger, gone. The new sea-wall
Efficiently controls the tides until
They
Get around to abolishing the strand
Altogether, entirely, shortly.

Slowly, night comes to Sandymount,
Soon like Horan's field to be abolished also
When the land is sold, the old
Victorian and Edwardian modest
Family houses demolished,
Making way for tall stately
Office blocks,
Their square skulls
Gazing out confidently to the retreated sea,

The village, like childhood, only remembered
By old faded photographs.

Marise . . . .

Uncollected
poems

WATERFORD

(For Violette)

A friendly town. Even the prim pylons gibber
Their enormous welcome as the train moves in
To the rock defile that is the station. Here
The streets lean back like girls for the traveller's kiss

As he runs from his guilt to seek refuge among
The dead and the dying, the forgotten, the lost, the unknown:
For there is peace in this place in our time, apparently, though eyes
Are veiled, concealing what secrets, what something of sadness-

Regret for the, alas, so dead? But, constructed in ten-o-three
By Reginald, burly and blond, a Danish keep still stands
By the Suir water's edge, to remind the Irish here
Of a life alien to theirs and hostile. Yet not here,

Not in this city or environs do the great blond gods
Come grinning from the sea, sun on winged helmets shining
To demand their share of earth, their natural birthright,
Denied by the hearths where their youth was happy.

No, they are so, oh, dead; and their descendants here
Carry too death in their eyes and soft ways. Even this keep
From which Strongbow married a girl called Eve, a woman
For whom many a man sat down, retains no longer

The echo of laughs long gone, and not strife's despair,
Lancing the breast of the daring Norman, or sorrow's steel,
Tearing the eyes like damp cloth, has left a trace:
The bricks crumble. Decay is here like dogs.

And in these streets we walked, happy for ten days,
Forgetting our private agonies, our accustomed public grief,
Forgetting the days of the European dangers, half-wishing
The deliberate amnesia would be permanent like birds.

Yes, it was good: going with you down to the water,
Watching the nonchalant ships and the serious gulls.
On the hills, the trees nodded their benediction,
And the wet fish in the river swam home to our hands.

But this peace is not for us: it is an escape.
The seeds of our peace are where our agonies flower.
We must return to our empty smiles, to the hail-fellow-met
Of our consciousness, to the fear, the guilt of our gaiety.

But I will care for those days: they will be gears
In the mechanism of my mind as I travel the earth
Wishing, Violette, for your long jet hair,
And the lucid beauty of your classical face.

Poetry Ireland 1948

VARIATION ON A THEME (No.2)

When Patrick Pearse walked down the city
Mothers hid their children from his passing glance
And watched, with stern misgiving their grown sons
Following his day's red advance.

And when he piped them down the rose road of death
One Easter Monday in O'Connell Street
There was much silent and private lamentation
And grave talk of treason and deceit.

O what terminations of mortality
Weigh heavily on this man's head.
Will he have the courage to acknowledge them
On Mount St. Joseph when gather his dead.

(MSS. 30/31 1942)

POEM ('THIS IVORY-HANDLED KNIFE...')

This ivory-handled knife, handed down by our fathers,
Generation through generation, has lain long on the table,
Used only for opening envelopes or cutting paper.
A good while ago, I realised that its tapering
Point would probe something tougher, sometime investigate
A substance less malleable, not so smooth.
Note, now, time, place and other details. Be
Circumspect and, seizing a right opportunity,
Slit deliberately the throat of this slavering beast
Advancing upon us, letting the thick blood flow
That once a generation must discolour
Mind and heart and nestle behind the skull.
When you have killed it, tell me. I would want to know.

(Dolmen, 1962)

POEM ('RED-FACED...')

Red-faced with cauliflower hands
With the eyes of the idle-gazing
Needling me, stripped I stand
Tears troubling me daily.

The moons in my eyes wane not.
I am afraid of my mother.
The stone she gave me I forgot
– She loves not you: another.

She accepted my love like a bouquet,
Then ripped it, flung it down
I thought she was joking
I laughed; then quietly down

Down in my breast, a cat curled
And claws stretched in my heart's strings.
Everywhere eyes began
To focus me in their visioning

I am, a mountainous size.
On pedestal, awkward alone I stand,
Red-faced with cauliflower eyes
And a tear in my hand.

(MSS. undated)

LOVE AND HATE

Crossing the roadway in no uncertain fashion
I made for her doorway and without knocking
Entered the kitchen where she was scrubbing
The night from her eyes like any servant-girl.

The words spun in my eyes, reared behind my teeth,
Yet when I saw her I closed the door carefully,
And my hate sank behind my love like clouds
That are bundled over a mountain and pushed out of sight.

The Bell, 1955

NO DANCE TONIGHT AFTER ALL

Lady, the dancing is over. The musicians
Have all gone home. We have arrived too late

And it is disturbing to see the room exhausted,
Dishevelled like a girl after passion.

Put on again your bright blue cloak
Lined with ermine and quietly let us go too.

Lady, I thought we could have danced tonight.
I thought we could have been happy together with the music

But we have missed the party, and the bows' daredevil
Dance on the strings of the muted violins

The Bell, 1955

BY THE WATERS OF THE YAMUNA

Strange to us from the West, reared on hope
And ambition that like a green stalk ripens,
Wards of a temperate nurturing nature,
To watch these children their eyes filled
Not with despair – like hope here irrelevant –
But a dubious trust, each day renewed,
In simple survival, an oriental resignation sensing
Their ambition withered in this scruffled dust, their cradle.

In once-white see-through rays
Evidencing only an awareness of clothes,
With their sticks, stone chips, skipping ropes,
Skeletal hounds sniffing by garbage heaps
Under the beady eyes of the calm-eyed vulture,
That changes only its talon-grip, they play
By the stenching ghats on the corpse-ridden river
That flows to – well, anyway, somewhere:

How should they know, their lives
Bounded by poverty's territorial limits,
A couple of weary miles there and aridly back
– Searing travel under the jading sun –
To the parched hardly shaded pad
With its torpid burden of familiarity

('unfinished' MSS. undated)

Versions and translations

SEÁN Ó RÍORDÁIN

REO

Maidin sheaca ghabhas amach

FROZEN

On a frosty morning I went out
And a handkerchief faced me on a bush.
I reached to put it in my pocket
But it slid from me for it was frozen.
No living cloth jumped from my grasp
But a thing that died last night on a bush
And I went searching in my mind
Till I found the occasion's equivalent—
The day I kissed a woman of my kindred
And she in the coffin, frozen, stretched.

Poetry Ireland Review, 1955

SEÁN Ó RÍORDÁIN
ADHLACADH MO MHÁTHAR
Grían an Mheithimh in úllghort

MY MOTHER'S BURYING

A June sun in an orchard,
A rustle in the silk of afternoon,
The droning of an ill-natured bee
Loudly ripping the film of evening.

Reading an old dog-eared letter,
With every tearful word I drank in
A raging pain stabbed my side.
Every word forced out its own tear.

I remembered the hand that did the writing
A hand as familiar as a face,
A hand that dispersed kindness like an old Bible,
A hand that was like the balsam and you ill.

And June toppled backwards into Winter.
The orchard became a white graveyard by a river.
In the midst of the dumb whiteness all around me,
The dark hole screamed loudly in the snow.

The white of a young girl the day of her First Communion
The white of the holy water Sunday on the altar.
The white of milk slowly issuing from the breasts:
When they buried my mother—the white of the sward.

My mind was screwing itself endeavouring
To comprehend the interment to the full
When through the white tranquility gently flew
A robin, unconfused and unafraid.

It waited over the grave as though it knew
That the reason why it came was unknown to all
Save the person who was waiting in the coffin
And I was jealous of the unusual affinity.

The air of Heaven descended on that graveside,
A marvellous holy joy possessed the bird.
I was outside the mystery, a layman,
The grave before me in the distance.

My debauched soul was bathed in the waters of sorrow,
A snow of purity fell on my heart.
Now I will bury in my heart so made clean
The memory of the woman who carried me three seasons in her
    womb.

The gravediggers came with the rough noises of shovels
And vigorously swept the clay into the grave.
I looked the other way, a man was brushing his knees.
I looked at the priest, in his face was worldliness.

A June sun in an orchard.
A rustle in the silk of afternoon.
The droning of an ill-natured bee
Loudly ripping the film of evening.

Lame little verses being written by me.
I would like to catch a robin's tail.
I would like to rout the spirit of those knee-brushers.
I would like to journey sorrowfully to the day's end.

Poetry Ireland Review, 1955

RENÉ GUY CADOU
POEME D'AMOUR A HÉLÈNE

LOVE POEM TO HÉLÈNE

So I awaited you as one awaits the ships
In those arid years when the grain
Grows no higher than the blade of grass
Sensing with dread the dour season's menace.

I waited for you: while all the docks, the highways,
Reverberated to my ardent step that towards you
Moved — towards you in whom I am sustained
As by a gentle rain that never dies

And your only movement was of your eye-lashes
Like birds' feet drawn on frosted glass
I only saw in you that solitude
That placed its branching fingers on my neck.

And so in the dawn of my life
You were the morning cadences that awakened me
And all my birds, my vessels, my lands
My stars, those millions of stars which then arose.

Ah ! when you spoke, how all the windows
Sparkled in the evening like new wine
And the doors opened on the busy towns
Where we walked, arm in arm, along the roads.

And from so far away behind your countenance you came
That I did not know at each heart-beat
If I would live till you had arrived
Where you would be in me stronger than my blood.

Hélène ou le Règne Vegetal: Editions Pierre Seguers.
(Dolmen, 1962)

RENÉ GUY CADOU

'Celui qui entre par hasard dans la demeure d'un poète . . .'

(UNTITLED POEM)

He who by chance enters the poet's house
Does not know that the furniture has power over him
That each knot of wood embraces more
Of the cries of birds than the whole heart of the forest.
Suffice it that a lamp places its slender neck,
At the close of evening, in a varnished corner
Suddenly releasing a swarm of bees,
The odour of fresh bread, of cherry trees in blossom.
Such is the happiness of that loneliness
That a plain caress of the hand
Gives again to that heavy furniture, black and silent,
The lightness of a tree in the morning.

(ANON.)

PRIOSÚN CHLUAIN MEALA

Ó, bliain's lá amárach…

CLONMEL PRISON

O a year from tomorrow I left my own people,
I went down to Ardpatrick, the ribbons in my hat.
Some Whiteboys were there then, they were rustling cattle
And now I'm sad and lonely in Clonmel's foul prison.

My bridle and saddle are gone from me this long time,
My hurley well hidden behind my own door,
My slither's being played with by the boys of the valley
The one I could hit a goal with as good as another.

O Kerrymen, please pray for me, soft and lovely were your voices,
Little I thought ever that I never would return to you
And to think our three heads will be spiked and on show here
In the snows of the winter's night and any other weather that comes
     to us.

To Iveragh if you ever go, take the news to my people
That I'm lost to this world now and will be dead beyond Friday.
Make sure there's a good wake for me, a good coffin to carry me in:
That's the end of O'Donnell and forever say a prayer for him.

BRENDAN BEHAN

JACKEEN AG CAOINEADH NA mBLASCAOD

Beidh an fharraige mhór fé luí na gréine mar ghloine

THE BLASKETS

The great sea under the sun will lie like a mirror,
Not a boat sailing, not a living sign from a sinner,
The golden eagle aloft in the distance, the last
Vestige of life by the ruined abandoned Blaskets.

The sun will be gone, the shadow of night spreading
As the moon, rising, through a cloud coldly stretches
Its ghostly fingers over the silent earth
Where, wracked, the shells of the houses stand deserted

— Silent save for the birds all homeward flying
Glad to be back, their heads on their breasts lying.
And the wind soughing, softly a half-door swinging
By cold wet hearths, their fires forever extinguished.

BRENDAN BEHAN

THANKS BE TO JOYCE

Here in the rue St. Andre des Arts
In an Arab tavern, pissed,
For a studious Frenchman I construe you,
For ex-G.I.'s and a Russian, pissed.
All of those things you penned I praise
As, in France, I drink Pernod in return.
Proud of you as a writer we are
And grateful for the Calvados we owe to you.

If you were me
And I were you
Leaving Les Halles
Holding all this cognac
On a full belly bawling
You'd write a verse or two in my praise.

BRENDAN BEHAN

OSCAR

After all the strife
That, alive, he caused,
Ravaged with fear,
In the half-light stretched,
The gay spark's body
Lies dumb in the dark,
Silent, the funereal
Candles guttering,
The graceful body,
The firm gaze, spent
In a cold bare room
With a concierge spiteful
From too much attendance
On a foreign tippler
Who left without paying
The ten per cent service.
Exiled from the Flore
To a saintly desert
The young prince of sin
A withered churl
The gold jewel of lust
Left far behind him.
No Pernod to brace him
Only holy water
— The young king of Beauty,
A ravished narcissus
As the star of the pure Virgin
Glows on the water.

Envoi
Delightful the path of sin
But a holy death's a habit.
Good man yourself there, Oscar: Every way you had it.

From *BUILE SHUIBHNE (THE MADNESS OF SWEENEY*, medieval Irish)
Ba binne lium robháoi tan…

KING SWEENEY'S VALEDICTION

Suibhne or Sweeney, King of Dal Araidhe in Ireland, treacherously kills one
of St. Ronan's acolytes during the battle of Moira in A.D. 637. As a result of
St. Ronan's curse, Sweeney goes out of his mind and spends the rest of his life
wandering throughout Ireland stark naked and living in the trees. In his turn,
he is treacherously injured and, as he lies dying in the arms of St. Moling, he
makes this lay:

> Sweeter far to me once
> Than the tranquil conversing of my kindred,
> The churkling of the turtle-dove
> Swooping over the pool.
>
> Sweeter far to me once
> Than the sound of the prayer-bell beside me,
> The melody of the blackbird on the cliff,
> The stag belling in the tempest.
>
> Sweeter far to me once
> The howl of the wolf-pack
> Than the voice of the cleric within
> Lowing and bleating.
>
> Though you relished your pot-houses
> And your sumptuous ale-feasts,
> I preferred a draught of clear water
> Drunk from the palm out of a well.

Though sweet to you in your church there
The calm discoursing of your students,
Sweeter to me the pleasant paean
Sung by the hounds of Glen Bolcain.

Though you relished the salt meat and the fresh
Eaten in your assembly houses,
I preferred a fistful of fresh cress
Eaten somewhere carelessly.

The cruel herd's spear has wounded me
Travelling clean through my body.
A pity, O Christ who gives every judgement,
That I was not killed at Moira.

Though good every bed in truth
I made around Ireland,
I'd prefer a bed over the lake
In the open Mourne mountains.

Though good every bed in truth
I made around Ireland
I'd prefer the bed in the wood
That I made in Glen Bolcain.

I give thanks after that
For partaking, O Christ, of your body,
Truly repenting on earth
For every evil deed I have done.

(from the Irish)

GAIUS VALERIUS CATULLUS

CARMEN XI

Furius and Aurelius, buddies of Catullus,
Whether he is exploring the outer Indies
Where, constantly echoing, the appropriate seas
                Smash on the shore,

Or whether he is in the Near East among the shifty Arabs
Or in Central Asia among the well-heeled Parthians
Or where the seven-fingered Nile
                Massages the desert,

Or even if he goes over the frozen Alps
Viewing the marvellous work of the great Caesar
— Right along the Rhine and even among the really
                Unspeakable British,

My true friends, ready to face such specific dangers
Shoulder to shoulder with me, and even unknown other perils,
Are you ready now to take over to my girl-friend
                A short and bitter note:

May she live and rot with her lechers
And may she give three hundred of them some night
The same routine, leaving them all
                Burnt up the same way.

She need not, as long ago, worry about my love
Which she has killed herself — just as the flower
At the edge of the field by the plough
                Is savaged and abandoned.

Poems in Irish

IN MEMORIAM
Sheamais Mac Muircheartaigh
d'éag 5 Lunasa 1974

Is cuimhin liom an lá ud
Cúig bliana fichead ó shion
Agus sinn ag siúil maguaird an tsráid-bhaile
Nuair a dhírigh se a mhéar agus d'fiafraigh díom:
'Conas a ghlaofá san?' agus d'fhreagair mise:
'Imeall an phortaigh'. 'Ceart go leor', dúirt se
'Ach fadó nuair bhíomar ag oscailt phortaigh,
Fiacala an phortaigh a thugamar air'

Agus ba íomha shamhalta fíor é
Fód móna bainte amach annso a's annsud
Le sleanaibh. Fén chré dhó fein le fada
Séamas Mac Muircheartaigh as Baile an Fhirtéirigh,
Saoi, col cheatair mo chéile Síle Ní Mhainnín,
Saoi a mhúin dom de cheart-Ghaeilge a bhfuil agam.
Guiom sólás síorrai dí dhílseacht,
Dá chneastacht, da mheabhar gear oilte shaibhir

De Bhaile Átha Cliath dom-sa áit a d'fhoghliomaoís an Ghaeilge
Agus líon se go failtiúil na bearnacha im' imleabhar.
Cuimhníom go minic air agus na deochanna bhí againn
Gach oiche ar an mBuailtin um dheire lae —
An t-amhránaíocht i dtigh Ui Chatháin
Agus thar n-ais ina thigh féin an scéalaíocht
Fén sean-am nuair bhi se ina óige
Agus an bothantaíocht níos minic í na mar atá anois

Tairgim na linte seo dhó le buíochas,
Le ghrá agus cuimhne brónach
Go dtí go luighfidh me féin leis fén chré.
Ní bhead arís fén a dhíon i mBaile an Fhirtéirigh
Ró-aosta anois mé don taisteal fada chun a uaigh
Agus me féin ag triaill ar uaigh i mBaile Átha Cliath
Mar a bhfuil mo mhuintir curtha
Agus mar a cuirfear mise san triail deireannach.

IN MEMORIAM
Seamas Mac Muicheartaigh
Died 5 August 1974

I remember that day
twenty-five years ago
us walking around the town road
when he pointed his finger and asked me:
What do you call that?' And I replied:
'The edge of the bog.' 'Right enough', he said
'But in the old days when we opened the bog
We called it the teeth of the bog.'

And the fanciful image was true
The sod of turf dug out here and there
With slanes. Himself now beneath the clay this long time,
Séamas Mac Muicheartaigh from Ballyferriter
Wise man, cousin of my wife Sheila Manning,
Wise man who taught me what decent Irish I know.
I pray for eternal solace for his loyalty,
His kindness, his sharp, articulate, rich mind.

I was from Dublin, and that was where I learned Irish
And he generously filled the gaps in my knowledge.
I often remember him and the drinks we had
Every evening in An Buailtín at the end of the day -
The singing in O'Kane's
And afterwards in his own house, him telling
About the old times when he was in his youth
and the visiting among houses more often than now.

I offer these lines to him with gratitude,
With love and sorrowful memory
Until myself I'll be lying with him under the clay.
I will not be back beneath his roof in Ballyferriter
I'm too old now to travel far to his grave
And myself heading for the grave in Dublin
where my people are laid
And where myself will be laid in the last journey.

DÁN

Cúchulain, an fear glic san go raibh neart fíre ann
agus a chúl le cloch níorbh áil leis glórtha ban:
Ruathar fiolair fiáine thar a cheann annsan,
ionnsaí nimhneach dha imshuíomh le gathanna;

Agus anois an bheatha chródha san ag druidim chun a dheire
le rudaí tabhachta neamh-dhéanta aige tré ghnóthaí eile ag
brú air riamh, codhnachas smaointe, cogaí, mná,
maoin-chíocrach smachta Éireann uile dar thug sé grá;

agus anois níl féith ann chucha-san; trua go raibh riamh
ach níl dul siar air; trua, cheap sé, gur dóibh bhí iath
'na inntinn chomh fada san in ionad a theaghlach féin 'chothú.
Níos congaraí anois na fiolair a's an uaigh.

Ach b'fheidir gurab fhiú go léir é: a ainm 'dhul síos
'sa stair mar laoch neamheaglach, glan a choinsias,
gur chóimhlíon sé a dhualgaisí go réidh roimh suan.
Ná fiolair anois go réimh 'ghá mbunú.

Cúchulainn, that clever man that plenty of sincerity in him
with his back to a rock he had no wish for the sound of women's voices
a rush of wild eagles above his head there,
a deadly attack assailing him with darts.

And now that courageous life drawing to a close
with important things not done because other business
was always pressing him, mastery of thoughts, wars, women,
covetous of ruling all Ireland to which he gave his love;

and now he has no inclination for them; pity he ever had,
but it can't be undone; a pity, he thought, that for them he had room
In his mind for so long, instead of looking after his own household.
Nearer now are the eagles and the grave.

But maybe it was all worth it: his name to go down
in history as a fearless warrior, his conscience clear,
That he fulfilled his duties well before he slept.
The eagles now settling themselves already.

Wrap Up My Green Jacket

Verse play for radio, BBC Third Programme, 1947

WRAP UP MY GREEN JACKET

[Note from 1947 performances] :
This verse-feature, which deals with the tragedy of Robert Emmet and
Sarah Curran, was first broadcast in the BBC Home Service on February
3rd, and was repeated in the BBC Third Programme on May 26th. The cast
included Cyril Cusack, Betty Chancellor, Harry Hutchinson, Joan Plunkett
and Laidman Browne. Robert Irwin sang the 'Moore's Melodies' and Brian
George sang Mr. Iremonger's ballads to airs arranged by Sheila Manning.
Production was by Louis MacNeice.

> *FADE IN* 'Oh ! breathe not his name,' *Two verses—very soft.*

MAN : If you come this way. . . .
Which is the way you should come,
It's not far now. We're almost there.
If you stand here for a while, here by the hedge,
Leaning your head to one side a little, look :
Down there in the summer evening the city lies
Snug as a kitten curled by its mother's breast,
And there Rathfarnham by the river sleepily
Lazes in the sunshine ; and all around, the fields,
The rich earth, the land he loved. Again
The other way, the land he loved : Tibradden,
Kilmashogue, Larch Hill, Three Rock.

How many times did he, walking like us
On a spring evening past Marlay see
Among the wheat rows the Corn Marigold poke its head ;
Or see the long gold chalices of the first buttercups
Making each meadow an El Dorado. Look around now
For what we see to-day he in his turn saw

Almost one hundred and fifty years ago, the annual
Chronicles of nature written under the same sky,
In the same fields hedged by the self-same hills.

Upon the coping of that sundrenched wall
The Little Stitchwort's milkwhite head appears
Almost too heavy for the inch-high body.
The wild Bugle is in purple blossom and even
The small Wall-Saxifrage upon its unclothed stem
Sports dingy white bells. White, too, the blossoms
Of the Wild Strawberry, there on that sunny bank,
Sheltered by the kindly grass and among the Pepperwort,
    look
God's Cow, the Spotted Ladybird, seeks its insect prey.

Here too, the dragon-fly drones into summer
The Corncrake's strident voice calls from the lengthening
    grass
The Yellow Hammer assumes its summer station
And in the Hedge bannered with Snowy Blackthorn
The Bullfinch preens its rich red plumage.
To-night under the Love Moon the reckless beetle
In great whirling curves will bank, the bat on regular beat
Will police from end to end the orchard, the Badger
Hunt the new-seen hedgehog and the young rabbits
Meet their dread enemy, the slinking fox.

Nothing has changed since he was here walking
With springing step these rich green hills.
Nothing has changed since he was here talking
To his girl-friend of his country's ills.

Nothing—save what was man-made, an old house,
Perhaps, a coachroad, a pillared gate :
Refuges now for the grass and the field-mouse—
The living moral in the sad still fate.

You and I too like him and her will fall
Beneath the wheels of Time's great burning car,
Leaving nothing more than a name on a chapel wall
That time's long arm will even stretch to mar.

But nature, in a hundred years or more
With all this bright and twentieth century gone
Under this sun and the pulsating moon will roar
Through each year's archway, working on.

This, then, is the setting :
The fields where nature grimly works away ;
The impenetrable mountains steadily watching
The grave decline of each century ;
And crouched below them, dwarfed by their terrible
     importance
That Augustan city : where everything is a bit mad ;
Where everything goes wrong, becomes something else,
Something that wasn't meant at all ; or else,
More usual, fritters out ineptly ; the second city,
Once of a mighty empire, that still can't get the hang
Of its self-chosen new importance. Here was staged
Many of the scenes of the tragedy—or farce, depending
On the way you look at it : though
Underneath the tears lies always laughter, underneath the
     laughter, tears.

There now is the house : look ; or rather what's left of it
At this late hour of the day. See where the gables
Poke into the air, the chimneys crumble :
There's not much left now of all that grandeur.

Come with me ; over the ditch ;
And let us cross the meadow to the house
As Greenfinch and Goldcrest sing us into history.
Missel Thrush and Wagtail escorting us steadily
So did the birds these lovers in their evening walks
Attend while history congealed around them slowly,
Freezing their names in these everlasting hills.
Like flies in amber here they are forever :
An arrested gesture fixed in immortality.

So to the house the last few yards we cover.
The ground is broken with the cattle's hooves
Where once the coachroad ran towards the city.
Nothing but the walls remain of this fine house
And inside them, rubble : slate, brick and plaster,
Over which the grass is grimly working ;
And, look, in the garden, bindweed, dock and nettle,
Cowparsley and thistle riot. Desolation.
Nothing left of all that grandeur.
This, then, is the house we travelled out to see,
The house where Sarah Curran lived : the Priory.

GIRL : Sally Curran !

MAN : Yes, Sally Curran : a girl who loved a boy
Who loved a principle better than a girl.

GIRL: Sally Curran in her charm and beauty weeping
       By the river for her lover dead and gone,
       Weeping for her lover dead and gone.

MAN: Weeping for her lover dead and gone.
       A scatterbrain who, playing with fire, was burnt.

GIRL: Love for a woman is the beginning and end,
       Cause and effect, the why and the wherefore.
       For a man it is less than an ideal strung out in front of him
       A carrot slung before a donkey which he will chase
       And never reach but keep on chasing.
       So will a woman interest herself in what her lover
       Does yet her mind and instinct's elsewhere,
       Rooted on earth, here, between the boundaries
       Of birth and death. And Sally Curran, talking
       Of revolution was little different from any other woman.

MAN: Anne Devlin, strung and restrung upon the gallows,
       Her dress torn and retorn with the yeomen's bayonets.

GIRL: Anne Devlin had no lover to distract her
       And Sally too was young, walking into the sunset
       Waiting for the evening to bring her lover to her
       To pace these grounds with her and talk his wild talk.

MAN: His wild talk had weight behind it.
       Never was a revolution so well organised
       And never did anything fritter out so farcically.

GIRL: Was he right or wrong to attempt revolt
       And draw the hangman's axe upon his neck

And on the necks of others too?

MAN : We'll never know.
Too many circumstances condition the answer
And it's now too long ago to judge fairly.
Our mental atmosphere has changed too much.
You and I, who grew up in a free country,
Whose eyes look further than England, out to Europe,
To the world, cannot really know what it meant
To be cramped under a yoke like oxen.
We, in our independence, deal freely in concepts ;
They, manacled, could only know their bonds.
And so we're hard on them and the bitter word
The jibe, is oftener in our mouths than praise.
Yet if only these stones could speak. . . .

GIRL : If only these stones could speak. . . .
Stone, stone, speak to me.
Tell us what you once did see
When Robert Emmet and his love
Walked, the bright sun high above.

Interpretation's but a game
Two can play at, just the same.
And if the angle we take's hard
Your audience will mark their cards

One up for Emmet who could dare
To die bravely, head in air,
And one for Sally, left alone,
Heart as dead as a dead stone.

Stone, stone, speak to me.
Tell us what you once did see
When Robert Emmet and his love
Walked, the bright sun high above.

*   *   *

ROBERT : Sally . . . Sally, what are you doing there at the window?

SALLY : Nothing.

ROBERT : Something's the matter. I can't follow your gaze.
Although you're staring out you're not looking at anything.
Whatever your eyes see, it's not those hills
That crooked tree or the golden-carpeted fields.

SALLY : Oh ! Robert ! Robert !

ROBERT : What is it, Sally ?

SALLY : My father has forbidden me to see you : Oh ! not directly,
He said nothing to me ; but my sister Amelia
Says that he hinted your visits should be
Less frequent. He says you're dangerous
And will not hear of you as a suitor for me.

ROBERT : I see. And you, what do you say?

SALLY : The wealth that I seek is one fair kind glance from my love.
Oh ! Robert, these last few days I had intended
To write and tell you ; but anything like consolation
I should be unable to convey ; so I thought I'd wait

And kiss the hurt away as soon as done.
Twice to-day I passed the house you're in
But did not see you.

ROBERT : Little time I have to look at the thousand difficulties
That lie between me and the completion of my wishes.
That they shall disappear I have evident and rational hopes.
God having gifted me with a sanguine disposition,
I run from reflection ; if beneath my feet a precipice
Opens, from which my duty will not suffer me to shrink
I should be grateful for being thrown down,
My eyes still fixed on the visions of happiness
My fancy formed in the air. Let's not be sad, Sally.
Things will be all right when Summer flicks over
A new page in our lives and in Ireland's history.

SALLY : If I thought you were safe I should be
Comparatively happy ; but this uncertainty
Makes me uneasy : I cannot be still
Though my heart cries out for quietness.
I derive more consolation from
Your scribbled notes than from any effort
Of reason on my mind. I know now
We must try to forget the past and fancy
Everything is to be attempted for the first time. . .
How are your plans ? Is everything ready ?

ROBERT : Almost. I believe that when Autumn's candles
Flame out on every tree, a new chapter will be added
To the long story we are familiar with already.
Nothing has been left to chance ; to the last detail
Everything has been organised and plans of campaign

For street fighting behind barricades worked out
In case our first swift stroke fails to take the Castle.
And if the French should land, either in England or
    Ireland,
Making sufficient diversion to distract the British
Success for our arms cannot at all be doubted.

SALLY : You are so confident. Does no doubt strike suddenly
    Ever into your brain, like a footpad in the night?

ROBERT : Doubts ? Yes, sometimes. Russell to-day
    Said this conspiracy was the work of the enemy.
    Such statements would shake the stoutest faith.
    Yet I don't believe it. We have been extra careful
    That secrecy like a black cloak cover all we did.

SALLY : Yet if by any chance, any accident . . . Oh ! What misery
    For the poor people. You know how cruel they are.

ROBERT : Yes. . . I have not forgotten the pitchcapped wretches
    Of Ninety Eight. Yet one grand point will be gained by *us*.
    No leading Catholic is committed with us, their cause
    Will not be compromised, we being all Protestants.
    And it is something to be sure of that one thing.

SALLY : You have the quality to relieve my mind
    I drown so much in your confidence. Yet at night
    Lying in bed while the moonlight steals
    Sideways into my room as into a church
    Doubts like grey ghosts come wandering through my
        head ;
    And I seem to see the bright flower of our love

Shattered by the sudden heavy stroke of a swift wind.
Sometimes I cannot stop the run of tears that flush
Suddenly down my cheeks when I see the future
Like a road stretching away, nothing to be seen on it,
Being blacked out by the tangled growth above it.
And I wish we were like other lovers, secure, content,
Sheltered by the branches of our families' approval,
Waiting calmly for the day when we could marry and be
    happy.
But always this country, trailing its cartload of sorrows,
Arranges the lives of its sons and daughters,
Comes between the girl and her lover like a thick
Curtain in whose folds they smother. Oh ! I'm sometimes
    angry
We allow it happen again and again, allow the dead
Stand up and dictate to us what we should do.
The dead. . . .

They walk in our gardens with their faces full
To the sunlight. Part the branches of trees
And you will find them there, crouching, eating
Our fruit. Even in our outhouses they huddle,
These armies that are not ours, that we do not
    acknowledge.

They have forced the doors of our houses, clambered in
Through the windows also. They roam through our rooms,
Lords of the manor. They have established outposts
Even in our attics. Their captains lounge in our chairs,
Smoking our best cigars and drinking our wines.

These cold soldiers have possessed our homes with
    arrogance,
Eyeing our babies, coveting our children, kidnapping
our young men,
Even seducing our wives. Look ! from the trees they hang,
Ghouls with the faces of men, jeering the passers-by
Or shadowing them through the streets for a new
    conquest !

Our hearts are swollen with our huge resentment.
By day we are not alone and in the waist of the night
They gather at our bedsides to disturb our sleep
With their long-eyed moaning, their banshee wailing,
Their sharp directions and their cutting words.
Ireland, talk to your dead ! Tell them we don't sleep at
    nights
Tell them we know that we've got to get back into Europe.
But say this is a land for the living, the dead cannot
claim it
Order them back to their serried graves, these phantoms,
Who are disturbing constantly our short lives' ease and
    peace.

ROBERT : Yet even you, Sally, *know* we cannot rest
        Till these things are readied once for all.

SALLY : Yes, I know. I'm sorry, Robert. It's hard
        Sometimes, that's all : especially when I remember
        That first evening of our love, not so long ago,
        When everything seemed perfect. Remember, Robert ?

ROBERT : Yes, I remember. . . .

All evening, while the summer trees were crying
Their sudden realisation of the spring's sad death,
Somewhere a clock was ticking and we heard it here
In the sunporch where we sat so long, buying
Thoughts for a penny from each other. Near
Enough it was and loud to make us talk beneath our
     breath.

And a time for quiet talking it was, to be sure, although
The rain would have drowned the sound of our combined
     voices.
The spring of our youth that night suddenly dried
And summer filled the veins of our lives like slow
Water into creeks edging. Like the trees, you cried.
Autumn and winter, you said, had so many disguises

And how could we be always on the watch to plot
A true perspective for each minute's value. I couldn't reply,
So many of my days toppled into the past unnoticed.
Silence like sorrow multiplied around you, a lot
Of whose days counted so much. My heart revolted
That time for you should be such a treacherous ally

And though midnight inclining bells over the city
With a shower of sound like tambourines of Spain
Gay in the teeth of the night air, I thought
Of someone who said the truth was in the pity,
Somehow, under the night's punched curtain, I was lost.
I only knew the pity and the pain.

*Fade in song softly in background. 'Believe me if all . . .' One
     verse. Fade to marching feet.*

Knock. Pause. A cry of fright.

VOICE B : Oh ! the police.

SIRR : I hold this house for our lord, the king. What's your name, please ?

Footsteps.

ROBERT : Cunningham.

SIRR : How long have you been here ?

ROBERT : I came only this morning.

SIRR : I see. Stay here, Walker, while I go upstairs.

Music.

SIRR : Mrs. Palmer, I am Major Sirr, from the Castle. What is your lodger's name, please ?

PALMER : Mr. Hewitt.

SIRR : How long has he been here ?

PALMER : He has been here several weeks.

Music.

VOICE : Dublin Castle, September 20, 1803. Sir, the trial of Emmet, which was brought forward yesterday, terminated as there was every reason to conclude in a conviction upon the clearest and most satisfactory evidence ; and it is universally admitted that a more complete case of treason was never stated in a court of justice. He produced no witnesses and made no defence. After the verdict of guilty was pronounced by the jury he was permitted to address the court before the passing of the sentence. He was more than once interrupted by the judge and was prevented from proceeding to the conclusion of his speech which appeared rather calculated to excite the indignation than the pity of those present. Sir, I have the honour to be your most humble and obedient servant, Hardwicke, Lord Lieutenant of Ireland.

VOICE C : What is your name ?

ROBERT : Robert Emmet. Having now answered to my name, I must decline answering any further questions.

VOICE C : You were sent for, Mr Emmet, so that you might have an opportunity of explaining what appeared suspicious in your late conduct.

ROBERT : I am sure it is meant to give me the opportunity and I am much obliged, but I must persist in declining. At the same time, I would wish it to be understood that there is nothing which could come within the limits of this society to which I cannot answer with pride. If I answer one, however, and not others, I would draw an invidious distinction which I do not wish to do.

VOICE D : When did you first hear of the Insurrection?

ROBERT : I decline answering any questions.

VOICE D : Did you see a proclamation purporting to be a
                 proclamation of the Provisional Government?

ROBERT : I have only to make the same answer.

VOICE D : Have you seen the same in manuscript?
                 Have you seen the same in your own handwriting?
                 Are you acquainted with Howley?
                 Why did you change your clothes?
                 Have you gone by the name of Hewitt? Ellis?
                     Cunningham?

VOICE E : Try Mr Emmet with these.

VOICE D : By whom were the letters written that were found on your
                 person?

ROBERT : As to the letters taken out of my possession by Major Sirr,
                 how can I avoid them being brought forward ? May I ask if
                 the name of the writer might be mentioned to me ? May I
                 know by what means these letters may be prevented from
                 coming forward ?
                 Has anything been done in consequence of those letters
                 being taken ?
                 May I learn what has been done upon them ?

VOICE D : You cannot be answered as to this.

ROBERT : You must be sensible, gentlemen, how disagreeable it
                 would be to one of yourselves to have a delicate and

virtuous female brought into notice. Might the passages in those letters be read to me ?

VOICE D : The expressions in those letters go far beyond a confidential communication between a gentleman and a lady. There are evidences of high treason, and therefore their production is necessary.

ROBERT : May I not be told the utmost limit to go to prevent the exposure ?
Then nothing remains to be done. I would rather give up my own life than injure another person.

VOICE D : We knew before you came into the room that this was the line you would take.

ROBERT : I am glad you have that opinion of me. May I know whether anything has been done ? May I then make one request—that until my arraignment nothing has and nothing will be done ?

VOICE D : You are at liberty to make the request but cannot receive an immediate answer.

ROBERT : Personal safety I throw out of the question. With notions of honour in common, persons may have different principles, but all I trust might be agreed as to what a person might owe to a female.

VOICE D : Are you aware that they form evidence against the person who wrote them ?

ROBERT :   As to that, I do not know how far there can be proof as
           to who wrote them, however there may be opinions. The
           production of these letters is the only act of my life, within
           these five months of which I have to accuse myself.

VOICE D : Do you mean that the person who wrote these letters only
           had opinions ?

ROBERT :   I say it on my honour. I only say that a woman's sentiments
           are only opinions and never reality. When a man gives
           opinions, it is supposed he has acted accordingly but with
           a woman the utmost limit is only opinion. I decide on
           my honour that the person had only opinions. I admit in
           the eyes of the law it is otherwise, but they may have laid
           down the law where it is not necessary. The same sword
           cuts down a man as a babe, but it is the mind of man
           which teaches him how to use it.

VOICE D : As a matter of curiosity I may put to you a question— why
           the government should indulge you with consenting to a
           partial disclosure of these letters when you decline on your
           part to make any satisfactory answer ?

ROBERT :   It is not an indulgence. I only ask it as if I was in a
           situation of power I would grant a like request. I wish
           everyone in Ireland and England was as innocent as she is.

VOICE D : Mr. Emmet's feelings are a good deal affected.

ROBERT :   I wish they were at an end. I wish you good morning,
           gentlemen.

VOICE D : Take Mr. Emmet away.

*   *   *

ROBERT : Six steps.
          Six steps.
          Twenty-four square yards, a chair and a plank bed,
          Usher me now into eternity. Receive me, O Lord,
          To-morrow when Dawn struggles over the eastern sky
          Cutting its capers over the glad earth and rippling sea,
          Poking through the narrow windows of the labourers'
              cottages
          And the great windows of Leinster House,
          Yet bringing me only another and final death
          Besides the many I die to-night.
          The Lord's my shepherd. I shall not want.
          He makes me to lie down in green pastures. . . .
          Green pastures. . . . oh ! Rathfarnham : Sally, Sally,
          Now are the thumbscrews of fate jammed down
          Upon our young and innocent love.
          Sir, keep her safely. She is young and good.
          Give her grace to withstand this trial of sorrow
          I have brought upon her and others—

ECHO : You admit it then?

ROBERT : What's that? What's that, I say?
          Damn you, answer. The cell is empty
          Yet I swear I heard a voice beside me.

ECHO : I said, you admit it then?

ROBERT : There I knew it. Yet
        There's no one there. Am I going mad?

ECHO : And well you might. But not yet.
       Have you answered my question?

ROBERT : Who are you? Damn it, who are you?

ECHO : Alter ego. Doppelgänger. Or just plain Conscience.
       You know you had to meet me?

ROBERT : I suppose so.

ECHO : I run from reflection, you said. Poor foolish boy,
       Alight with the arrogance of youth, the pride
       Of dreamt-of perfection. You run from reflection :
       But you can't run forever ; sooner or later, here or there.
       Somewhere or anywhere I catch up with everybody,
       Nobody escapes, nobody at all. From the highest in the
           land
       To the lowest, all must listen in the end
       To my sombre, deliberate voice.

ROBERT : I suppose so. *My* race is run, the grave
        Opens to receive me. I sink into its bosom.
        Will you not leave me alone now
        This last sad, still and lonely night ?

ECHO : Now above all is the time we must talk,
       The time for the cutting question and the hesitating answer,
       The time for the hedgings, the delaying tactics,

The smooth smilings, the long involved explanations :
'I meant this,' or 'I meant this,'
Or 'This wasn't what I meant at all,'
'It was this,' or 'It was this.'
And all the time like a relentless hound I pursue
You down the winding laneways of your explanations,
In and out, ducking and twisting but following you
Always, always and ever. Now is the time,
Now there is no other : for to-morrow in the dawn
You will have gone where I cannot reach you.

ROBERT : What is it you want ?

ECHO : One simple question I have asked and already
You evade it. I asked if you admitted it
The trial of sorrow, as you called it
You brought on this already unfortunate country ?

ROBERT : The cause was noble.

ECHO : A noble cause. Many a noble cause
Has forced men into an early grave.

ROBERT : I was right. I know it.

ECHO : You were right. Do you remember this –
Marching out at the head of that small band,
A brave, perhaps, but a foolish gesture ?
Listen. . . . Flash back your mind.

ROBERT : Men, we can wait no longer. Small as our force is, we may
yet catch them unawares and perhaps accomplish some

part of our original plan. Had I another week, had I one thousand pounds, had I one thousand men, I would have feared nothing. Yet we cannot now die cooped up in a trap. We'll take the Castle. March. . . .

ECHO: And down the street went Emmet's men To die in the foggy dew.
And you remember. . . . Kilwarden ?

ROBERT: Kilwarden ! Yes. . . . it was ghastly. . . .

ECHO: The justest judge in Ireland hanging from a patriot's pike.

ROBERT: I couldn't help it. . . . I called out :

ECHO: Yes, you called out—

Crowd Noise.

ROBERT: Stop it. Stop it, for God's sake. This is not an insurrection, it is a murderous riot. Get away as quickly as you can out of the city, out to the mountains. . . .

VOICE: Coward !

ROBERT: I'm not a coward, but this can't go on. I hadn't meant this at all. . . . Have my captains and my ministers departed. . . . Murder is no part of the plan. . . . Come on. . . . get away. . . . get away. . . .

ECHO: It was beyond what was calculated.
You planned the details well, everything

Worked out magnificently on paper—everything
Except human nature. That was something
You had not dreamt of in your calculations,
Being young and flummoxed with abstract theories.

ROBERT : Is that a crime—to be flummoxed with theories ?

ECHO : Is that a crime ? Not if your theories '
Be confined within the limits of your study,
Not if they be safe on paper. What
If your theorising and playing at revolution
Turn out as it turned out ? Those people,
But for you never had rioted,
And brought the soldiery upon themselves.

ROBERT : Something had to be done.

ECHO : Murder was done and will be done. Will your execution
Prevent the persecution of the people, will it
Be full atonement in the eyes of the law ?

ROBERT : I don't suppose so. Yet I thought of that too.

ECHO : You thought of that, too ; and, undeterred,
You led your men out down Thomas Street,
A handful of ragged turncocks and a few
Leaders in their bright green uniforms.
Commander-in-chief of the Forces of the Republic.
Sometimes, I can't help laughing.

ROBERT : Well. Laugh away. It was necessary.
Something had to be done and but for the accidental

Explosion in my depots, all had been well.
To rid my country of this execrable government
Foreign and oppressive, was what I wished,
As any man, no matter where he be, would wish.
Liberty –

ECHO : Liberty ! Ah ! I knew it would come.
And is liberty worth the shedding
Of a drop of human blood ?
Has a man not the right to accept his chains
In order that he may live till nature stops him ?
Is there no pride in defeat ?

ROBERT : Yes. But it is the pride that smoulders
Till it one day blazes out in flame
If by my action many were killed
And yet, as a result, one man were free,
I should consider my actions justified.

ECHO : One man ?

ROBERT : Yes, one man. One man with pride so great
The angels might weep sadly for him.

ECHO : Some men were killed there in Thomas Street
And who shall the angels weep for ?
Yes, they died.

VOICES : Bring him in. There, that's it. Put him down. Softly.
Don't jog him. Is he hurted ? Is he hurted badly ? How did
it happen ? O God, this is awful. Joe, are you all right, Joe ?

JOE :   Yes.

VOICE :   Is there anything we can do, Joe ? Joe, is there anything we
          can do ?

Joe sings the following to the air : 'Spailpín a Ruin.'

JOE :   Wrap up my green jacket in a brown paper parcel
        I won't need it now any more,
        Now the harp on the green standard low in the dust
        Lies covered with mud and with gore,
        For deep shall I lie who fell as the flag
        Fluttered down on the street and goodbye,
        Sweet goodbye to the Oul' Cause we cherished so long
        We bade with a heart-breaking sigh.

        O long by the Liffey I lived out my life,
        Minding children and house and fair wife,
        Till Kathleen Mavourneen called out and one day
        Closed down on the lease on my life
        And now in the foggy dew, dying, I lie
        Regretting the dawn I won't see,
        As slowly my life-blood stains the brown earth
        And slowly my life ebbs from me.

        While down from the high cliffs the rivulets teeming
        Are calling me sadly away
        Oh ! never again in this world shall I see
        The break of a new summer's day.
        So, as shines the bright sun and the old flag of green
        Floats not in the breeze as of yore,
        Wrap up my green jacket in a brown paper parcel,

I won't need it now any more.

ECHO :   So you see. Not everyone wished to die.

ROBERT :   Yet they'd do it again.

ECHO :   They'd do it again.

ROBERT :   You see. Something beside the mere desire to live
          Stirs always in the human breast.

ECHO :   And that is –

ROBERT :   Love : irrational and invincible.
          That stops the sun turning ;
          Makes the days aortas of joy ;
          Stiffens each weakening resolution.
          Love of this or of that—anything
          At all may start its swift race. . . .

ECHO :   Poor boy.

ROBERT :   Why do you say that ?

ECHO :   I thought of Sally Curran ;
          Sally Curran in love.
          Poor, poor Sally.

ROBERT :   Poor, poor Sally. What's happened ?
          Damn you, tell me what's happened ?

ECHO :   You tried to smuggle a note out to her ?

ROBERT :   Well. . . .

ECHO :   Foolish boy. . . .

ROBERT :   She's not in prison ?

ECHO :   No, not in prison. . . . When Major Sirr arrived
At the Priory to arrest her,
Sally
Went mad. . . .

ROBERT :   Sally, mad. . . . How am I expected to bear this . . .
Oh ! Sally, black-haired Sally with the laughing eyes
Now, indeed, the first barbed dart of remorse
Cuts into my heart and I am overcome.
Brightly in the evening I can see us walking
Not so long ago out by Larch Hill
Happy as the day was long and the sun
High in the sky. And, oh ! her lips were choirs
Chanting in my heart and head
And all the bright summer was a song sung by angels
Thick in the sky to guard us.
Softly down the roads of my being she wandered
As everything in me centred in to her
And she became the reason and the deed,
The question and the answer.
And under the trees walking in the summer
Everything seemed complete and in harmony,
And nothing else, nothing in the wide and alien
World mattered to either of us in our happiness.
Yet when I was away from her I could not forget
A whole nation crouching under a foreign flail

Being hammered back into the rich clay
Already so fertile with corpses –

ECHO :   Poor Robert ! Had you been older you had known better
The strength and meaning of the personal tie,
How everything else is of subordinate significance,
And smaller meaning, paling into nothing when set beside
This love of man for woman, woman for man.
This personal relationship between man and woman
In its strength and durability is a symbol
Of the relationship between man and God.
And surely Sally, black-haired Sally with the laughing eyes,
Was worth the whole of Ireland out to the four waves.
Think of her waiting under the evening sun,
A smile on her small face as she eagerly watched
The road for your approach. Think of her hair
Black as the darkest night, dancing under your fingers,
Her lips parting for your kiss . . .

ROBERT :   Stop. Stop. I can't bear it. I can't, I tell you. Go away, can't
you, go away. I don't want to listen to you. I was right, I
know I was. You're only here to torment me.

ECHO :   Love, you said, irrational and invincible –

ROBERT :   I won't listen to you. I won't, I won't. A devil from hell, that's
what you are. O my head. Why don't you go away ? Go
away. Go away. O God, I can't bear it. My head, my head . .
. Those shadows, what are they doing here ? . . . Send them
away. . . . Say Mr. Emmet is not available just now. . . . Do
you hear me ? Send them away. O I'm going mad. . . .

ECHO :   No, Robert, poor, poor Robert. ... You're not going mad.
         These are the things you raised yourself.
         Can't you hear them, hear what they're saying ?

         Fade in Violin : 'Bold Robert Emmet.'

DRUNKEN AND MOCKING VOICES :
         Fiach MacHugh has given the word
         Follow me up to Carlow.
         Solomon, where is thy throne. It is gone with the wind.
         Sarsfield is the word and Sarsfield is the man.
         I know U. I know N. I know I. I know T. I know E.
         I know D.
         United. United. United who ?
         United we stand and divided we fall.
         Ireland sober is Ireland free.

         Air : The Foggy Dew.

         The moon shone down on Dublin town
         On Sackville Street and the Coombe
         Its light hung over the Liffeyside
         Like a harbinger of doom.
         And in the West the sun glowing red
         Dissolved like a fading dream
         As down the street Bob Emmet's men
         Came marching in their jackets green.

         Tell me not in mournful numbers
         Rise, Arch of the Ocean and Queen of the West.
         Oh ! Robert ! Robert !
         Golden lads and lasses must like chimney sweepers come
             to dust.

O my Dark Rosaleen, do not sigh, do not weep.

Bold Robert Emmet, the darling of Erin,
Bold Robert Emmet, he died with a smile,
Farewell companions, both loyal and daring,
I'll lay down my life for the Emerald Isle.

Fill them up again there, Mick, and give the boys a pint a
    piece.

Air : Finnegan's Wake.

Oh ! Kitty Hooligan rising up one day
Said : 'Have you got your pikes, boys, now ?
I've got a flag, will you rally round it ?
Many a brave lad lies below
In his green and gold uniform he loved so
Much, wrapped in the cool, cool clay,
Happy and glad to die for my sake
No matter how sunny or long the day.'

But 'Kitty, my girl,' says I, 'you can keep
Your flags and your pikes and your coats of green.
Many a brave lad died for your sake
But take it from me that I'll not kneel
To you while the sun on the mountains the glad eye
Cocks at me, calling me to come and hear
Down the lanes of the spring and the leaf-ridden summer
The burst of life, blazing loud and clear.'

Have my captains and my ministers departed ?

Wrap up my green'jacket in a brown paper parcel
I won't need it now any more.

I met murder on the way he wore a mask like
Castlereagh.
Robert ! Robert !
The Lord's my shepherd. I shall not want
He makes me to lie down in green pastures.
Insurrection. . . . Ha !
Rebellion. . . . Ha ! Ha !
Revolution. . . . Ha ! Ha ! Ha !

ROBERT : I do not fear to approach the Omnipotent God to answer
for the conduct of my short life. Let not then any man
attaint my memory by believing that I could have hoped to
give freedom to my country by betraying the sacred cause
of Liberty. . . . Oh ! I'm tired. I wish I could rest. . . . I want
sleep. . . . Who are you, sir ?

DEATH : You want sleep. He is not to be had now. I, however, am
the brother of sleep.
People have been good enough to speak kindly of me from
time to time.

ROBERT : Death ?

DEATH : Yes, I am death. Now as I stare you in the face
Try, Robert, to compose yourself. I shall come
In the morning with a new day, calling for you,
Calling, 'Robert, come with me, come with me,
It's all right now.' It's all right now, if ever.
No need to worry about the rights and wrongs
Right or wrong prevailing, only I now remain

To greet you with a smile of welcome.

ROBERT : Yes, I know that. All is resolved now
At least as far as I'm concerned.
Always I thought, lying in bed at night,
Thinking of this or that, how I've enjoyed
That day or this, how I'd fear to meet you,
Particularly on the high road of my youth.
And now it seems you are not terrible at all
And you have a kind look in your eye.
I shall be glad to go with you when you call
At break of day to-morrow morning,
Out of this squalid cell, away from these iron jailers,
Saying goodbye to the clear blue sky and not crying.
I shall be thinking, perhaps, of Kilmashogue
Its shoulders curving under the evening sun.
And of the Priory sinking into the night's soft cushions.
Of the long fields that I know stretching into the sunset
And the long ribbons of roads reaching into the city. . . .
And Sally, I shall pray for, that these winds
Not break her. God grant she find some peace
Before another year rounds her life's corner.
And grant, if I have done her wrong, that she forgive me.
Come, Death, lie down with me to-night.
Stroke my head which is tired and aching.
Sing me a soft song that till to-morrow morning
I wait here, patiently. ... Sweet goodbye to everything
Now I give, forgiving my enemies
As I hope they forgive me. . . .

VOICE : This is the head of a traitor. . . .

Music and Song : '*She is far from the Land.*'